THE FUSION FAMILY

HOW TO SUCCEED WITH YOUR BLENDED FAMILY

CHARLOTTE EGEMAR KAABER

IUNIVERSE, INC.
BLOOMINGTON

The Fusion Family
How to Succeed with Your Blended Family

iUniverse books may be ordered through booksellers or by contacting:

iUniverse
1663 Liberty Drive
Bloomington, IN 47403
www.iuniverse.com
1-800-Authors (1-800-288-4677)

Because of the dynamic nature of the Internet, any Web addresses or links contained in this book may have changed since publication and may no longer be valid.

Any people depicted in stock imagery provided by Thinkstock are models, and such images are being used for illustrative purposes only.

Certain stock imagery © Thinkstock.

ISBN: 978-1-4502-7762-4 (sc)
ISBN: 978-1-4502-7763-1 (dj)
ISBN: 978-1-4502-7764-8 (ebk)

Library of Congress Control Number: 2010918353

Printed in the United States of America

iUniverse rev. date: 1/26/2011

CONTENTS

PREFACE

Holding this book The Fusion Family in your hand shows that you are aware of the challenges of being part of a blended family. You have decided to look for help and inspiration to succeed with your own family. I am very pleased with your decision and hope that this book can ease your way on a bumpy road.

The divorce rate is higher now than ever before, both in Europe and especially in the United States. In the United States one out of two marriages end in divorce. Sixty percent of second marriages fail, according to the U.S. Census Bureau 66% of marriages and co-habitation end in break up, when children are present, according to Stepfamily Foundation statistics.

Many blended families break up within the first year of co-habitating. Why do they give up?

Why is it so difficult? What went wrong?

What can you do to avoid becoming a part of this sad statistic? How can you prepare for and plan the best possible way for your blended family to succeed?

What kind of challenges, problems, and pitfalls will you encounter and how do you solve these issues within your blended family? How do you as a blended family stand in regard to your exes and their families, and society in general?

First, let me introduce you to my own blended family:

Charlotte fourty-two years old, Jégwan fourty-one years old, and our four kids: Oscar seventeen years old, Andrea fourteen years old, Nicklas fourteen years old, and Jonas eleven years old.

We live in Denmark, in a town called Slagelse, about 60 miles from Copenhagen.

We have been a blended family now for seven years. Our experience with the many challenges we have encountered, and also discussed with other fusion families, is described in this book. We would now like to share these experiences with you.

We have the children fifty percent of the time. Both Jégwan and I commute a lot, dropping off and picking up the kids. It is our priority to bring the kids together as much as possible.

Jégwan lost his heart to an old villa from 1921 which (still) needs a total renovation and a make-over (a slow and ongoing process.) Jégwan looks at it as his 'castle' and I see it as it-will-be-a-beautiful-home-in-ten-years. In the beginning I was frustrated on a regular basis, because of the slow process, but now I am (a bit) more relaxed and I am use to it.

Jégwan and I do Tae kwon do with the kids once a week. Half of my family enjoys spear fishing and spend many hours in the ocean. I only participate in the cooking part.

I think our four kids are cool. Oscar is very passionate about renovating stuff and spear fishing. Jégwan and Oscar have watched every single movie on this subject on YouTube.

Andrea is very good at playing the guitar. When I am in the living room downstairs, I can hear her from her room upstairs. It is very joyful.

Nicklas loves and knows everything about military stuff. Give him a weapon and he can fill your in on the details. He planned his military future when he was teen years old.

Jonas loves to watch the black belt coach Ehsan Fazli doing Tae kwon do, play his PlayStation 3 and his Wii with his friends. I was very surprised, when he told me that he had learned about meditation from one of his games.

With this book, we hope to inspire and help people who are entering into or who are already in a blended family-especially the single person with kids who meets a new partner and the person without kids who meets a new partner with kids. We will also discuss parents who would like to move in together and families that are already blended. We will also offer advice towards solutions of specific problems and inspiration for a less bumpy road towards success in your blended family.

How do you refer to your partner's kids? How do you refer to yourself with regard to them?

We say "fusion kids" and our new roles as "fusion parents." "Step" is NOT a part of our vocabulary; neither is the phrase "bonus kid" which is commonly used in Denmark. We made the conscious choice to use the word "fusion" instead of "step". The word fusion makes us both smile because we think the word is humorous, descriptive, objective, and up-to-date in a time of increased fusion by companies etc. Think about all the energy created by the fusion of atoms!

Our hope is that people refer to us as a The Danish Fusion Family – a real Atom Family. We spiced up this book with our own experiences and reflections. There are also interviews and effective coaching tools.

We also hope you read this book from beginning to end, since it is written chronologically by time events and includes a diverse set of problems and challenges you may encounter in your own blended family. Our book can also be used as a reference book, if you prefer.

Enjoy!
Charlotte Egemar Kaaber and Jegwan Kaaber

1. INTRODUCTION

The blended family, often including two sets of kids and respective exes, is almost as common as the "nuclear" family. Hurt feelings, jealousy, feelings of guilt, pick-up scheduling, exes, finances, up-bringing issues, habits, traditions – these are all part of the baggage, you accept when you blend families.

I think a lot of people realize that is it incredibly difficult and challenging to get a blended family to function well. The challenges are totally different from those in nuclear families. Complex emotions occur, some of which you never thought existed and therefore never had to deal with. It's a big personal challenge to become a fusion parent to another person's child and you will discover aspects of your own personality, you never knew you had before.

I hope when you read this book that you will smile, recognize yourself in the situations described, and think, "Yes, I have felt the same way." But most of all, I hope you will listen to your inner voice, which guides you true feelings.

In order to eliminate any confusion, I will define the terminology, I have used throughout this book:

The Fusion family is used instead of stepfamily.

Fusion mom/dad/kids are used instead of step mom/dad/kids.

The ex refers to previous partner or spouse.

The other parent is used by the kids to refer to their biological mom/dad.

The other parent household is used to describe the kids' biological mom/dad from whom you are divorced and her/his new partner.

The real parent is used when the fusion mom/dad is mentioned or compared to the biological mom/dad.

The parents are used as a common referral to the fusion parents and the parents in the blended family or for all the adults in both parent households.

2. I ONLY WANT MY PARTNER IN MY LIFE, NOT THE CHILDREN

There are many, both men and women, who at some point in their life have made a conscious decision not to have children and that children will not be a part of their lives. Often they find great value and quality of life in the freedom they have in their life. Therefore, it can be incredibly difficult for them when they meet "the one and only" and he/she has children.

Now for those of us who have children we may be tempted to think, that it is a part of your baggage and they just have to deal with it. But it is now that simple. Should you really have to give up in advance, when you finally found the right one? Imagine if you said that out loud: "I want nothing to do with my boyfriend's/girlfriend's children. Can you imagine the 'condemnation' you might receive? That's why you can not afford to say something like that or to feel that way. Where can you go and get help to deal with your conflicting emotions? Should you ask your partner with children NOT to see them or see them less often or should you ignore your feelings and just pretend while waiting for the kids to leave.

I do not think that will work out in the long run. Although it is a taboo subject it is about time we deal with it in a more solution-oriented way. Furthermore, I am a big believer that we all must fight for true love, when we finally meet it. So we should not just give up, although the situation seems intractable and does NOT disappear with time. Since I haven't found much guidance to the people caught in this dilemma, I want to give you a few pointers on how to deal with this antagonistic situation.

If you and your partner have this problem, you can choose to keep your own apartment. You stay in your own apartment, when your partner has his/her children visiting. Perhaps you feel an immediate strong opposition to this proposal, given that this is not a standard solution that fits in a defined family pattern. Maybe you can not imagine how you can have a close relationship if you and your partner do not live together. I think that you can. It is a question of maintaining the intimacy, even when you are apart.

If you do not like this proposal, you might try to keep track of how much time you spend on being annoyed by your partner's children. If it is too overwhelming for you, also mentally that you have to be with the kids in a few days, I think you should sleep on my proposal for a few days. Maybe it is a really good solution for you and your partner, when you can make yourself clear on how you feel and act accordingly.

If you, after having slept on my proposal, still feel that it just does not work for you, try to find a compromise. A compromise requires that you dig deep within yourself in order to find out what kind of emotions/values you feel that you have to "sacrify" by now having children in your life. Perhaps, you will realize that the "Feeling of freedom" is the most important thing for you to maintain. Then I subsequently would ask your, what in an everyday life with children, could give you that feeling as well. You might respond that you will feel freedom if you do not have to make sandwiches and washing the children's clothes.

Whatever gives you the feeling of freedom back even momentarily, please explain it to your partner. Your partner should now do the same exercise. He/she must find out how you can deal with the situation regarding the kids. How you can show that you are willing to take a step in his/her direction. Maybe your partner will suggest that you drop off and pick up children once a week.

If you choose the compromising path, then I obviously hope that it will be done wholeheartedly and without any martyr-like behavior. The 'Look-now-what-I-do-for-you' option does not work. Both you and your partner must make a decision about a compromise, which respects and takes each other's innermost values into account. And do try to remember to appreciate, respectively, the feeling of freedom and the feeling of helping each other out, when you decide to move forwards in the name of love.

3. BEFORE YOU MOVE IN TOGETHER – PLAN, ACCEPT AND COORDINATE

There are many things to consider when you meet someone who has kids, regardless of your own parental status. You have to decide if you want to buy the "whole package", which includes both your new partner AND their kids. And if you do want that, your responsibility to invest time in and give attention to your partner's kids is necessary, regardless of your feelings towards them.

Are you ready to take on the responsibility of becoming a parent to your partner's kids, even if you don't have any children of your own? Of course, the framework and content of your new role as a fusion parent is dependant on the ages of the kids. How do you see yourself in this role? How will you define it and what will it contain?

If you are a parent yourself, your greatest challenge is probably the upbringing of the kids and discovering how much "space" the kids will take in your respective lives as partners.

In this section I will make suggestions on how to plan and make it easier to get through this introductory phase towards a blended family life.

3.1   I'M GOING TO MEET MY PARTNER'S KIDS

If you have already met your partner's kids, you might recognize the situations described below.

If you have not met the kids yet, hopefully the following pages will give you an idea of how to handle the first few encounters.

The day has arrived and you and your partner have decided it's time to meet the kids. I'm sure you are tense and have memorized their ages, best friends' names, hobbies, what they like to do in their spare time, favourite food, etc. You are ready and extremely motivated for your first and most important investment in the process towards your new and blended life together.

If you have kids yourself, it's a good idea to have them stay at home or get a sitter for the first couple of times you meet your new partner's kids. Conduct the meetings outside your partner's home in a place where the kids will be independent of the adults and have a good time. Letting the meeting take place outside the home will reduce your feelings of obligation and might help to lessen your "stage fright." It will make you more relaxed, so you can be yourself and enjoy building the new relationship, being aware of all the impressions you will receive. You will feel less pressure to "perform."

When both you and your new partner feel comfortable with the results of these first meetings, you can then have the meetings take place at your partner's home, if possible. You will then be able to talk to the kids alone, see their rooms, and get to know them on their turf.

My own story

Many of you might recognize the above-described situation. I certainly remember the enormous demands and expectations that I put upon myself hoping to make a good impression on my new partner's kids. I tried to appear calm, enthusiastic, and extroverted, with a great sense of humor. However, deep inside I felt very nervous and had stage fright during the entire meeting. I was constantly evaluating the way things were playing out. My inner voice said "Relax, its just kids." However, I knew my relationship with the kids was paramount for a successful new blended family life.

The first meeting my kids, Nicklas and Jonas, had with my partner's kids, Oscar and Andrea, took place in my apartment. Jegwan and I planned this meeting in detail for weeks with everything coordinated and timed! The plan was that they would coincidently call to see if I would make them dinner that Friday. Fortunately, Oscar and Andrea liked the idea and they drove fifty miles to come to meet us. After the phone call, I felt the urge to pressure my kids to be on their best behaviour: share their toys, be fair, no interrupting or leaning over their plates while eating, etc. I also felt extreme stage fright on behalf of my boys-Nicklas and Jonas HAD to make a good impression on Oscar and Andrea. I remember that I even considered making them change their clothes, and almost asked them to change into light blue shirts, which looked really good on them.

Instead, I went into the kitchen and poured myself a glass of much-needed red wine. The plan was that I would make homemade burgers and have all the necessary condiments available in order to make this casual dinner a true success. In the end, Jegwan's son Oscar was very impressed by my knowledge of how-to-make-the-best-burger-ever. I just smiled and took in the compliments.

Reflection

In short, it really pays off to plan the first couple of meetings in detail, even if it feels awkward and staged. Why spend energy on dealing with grumpy kids, who don't like the food, when you can instead create calmness by planning ahead? I know from experience that it's better to get a head start by planning versus the possible stress you might otherwise feel during the first meetings. All that matters in the end is to leave a good impression.

3.2 LET'S PLAN AROUND THE KIDS: WHEN, HOW, AND WHAT DO WE SAY?

I can promise you one thing, planning a new blended family life is far from tedious. The process will be filled with signs pointing in different directions, but together you'll decide, which way is right for all of you. There will be issues to solve in order to create new arrangements or to adjust existing ones. If your blended family consists of two sets of kids, it's a good idea to consider changing or streamlining the arrangements of the time you spend together.

There are many different ways to arrange time together, with physical distance often being the deciding factor. The best way to do this is to have a set schedule, which helps both households and plan their lives accordingly.

My own story

Jegwan and I chose an alternative solution in scheduling time with the kids, due to the huge distance between homes and work places. Jegwan wanted to both be with his kids part time and also move in together, while I found that leaving my hometown with my kids difficult.

When planning around the kids, we prioritized having both sets of kids at the same time as the most important factor in our decision-making. We thought the best solution was to create only one kind of family constellation in order to make it easier for the kids. This constellation was now made of six people.

> **Reflection**
> I suggest having all the kids together at the same time if possible, even if it's only every other weekend. This way, the kids know what to expect and need only to relate to one kind of family constellation. Plus, if the two sets of kids get along really well, they will most likely prefer things this way and will make plans to spend time and play together

In considering the practical part of this solution, which included long commutes twice a week to pick up and drop off the kids, we made a conscious effort to make the drive for the kids something to look forward to. Our solution? We served warm Italian buns for the Friday morning commute, which made the long drive more attractive. The afternoon commutes are mostly spent chatting, and although we drive a lot it's all worth it in the end. This solution for time scheduling has worked out for our family. And today, Jonas feels it's only right, if we are all together at the same time.

3.3   CALENDAR PLANNING AND KID PLANNING: HOW TO PLAN

One way to plan is to have a schedule for an entire calendar year. Use two different colors – one for when the kids are at your house, the other for when they are with the other parent. Make sure to include all birthdays, holidays, and vacations so the kids know where they will spend their time. If possible, alternate between families on these important dates. Display the plan on the fridge, so everyone is clear about the schedule. It's even more effective if the other parent has an identical calendar plan displayed on their fridge.

> **Reflection**
> If you have younger kids, it's paramount to create such a plan in order to help them manage their fragmented life. This way they can visualize their schedule due to the color differences and ask questions if needed. It also gives them the opportunity to mentally prepare for any upcoming events, which eliminates disappointments and/or surprises of any kind.

3.4 WILLINGNESS TO TAKE RESPONSIBILITY

This topic is a "revolving door" both in my experience and in talking with other blended families. I can therefore conclude that it's a MUST that both parents take responsibility for each other's kids the same way they are responsible for their own kids. Whether or not the fusion parent is a parent himself or herself, this topic is an unquestionable requirement in making the choice to create a fusion family "package."

The role of a fusion parent demands an active and continuous effort, both in relation to the kids and to the real parent. The effort required is of course dependent on the age of the kids. If only one of you has kids, the biological parent will most often continue responsibility of all practical matters and up bringing. However, in other blended families, where both partners have kids, some choose to take responsibility only for their own biological kids. I know of many examples of the latter and conclude that this will NOT work out in the long run. There are several reasons why, which I will discuss later on in the book, including in the sub-section

5.4   Taking responsibility
5.4.1   "Just-wait-till-daddy-comes-home"

4. FUSION FAMILY MEMBERS BACKGROUND AND HISTORY

4.1 KNOWING AND ACCEPTING

From the very beginning, knowledge and acceptance is of paramount importance in how you deal with and handle issues in order to create the best foundation for a new life together. It's important that both of you are open and honest about relations and feelings. If you don't talk about these in the beginning, it could unnecessarily damage your blended life. I have created a list of issues, which could directly influence your new blended life and which are different from those of your own personal baggage:

1. 4.1.1   The kids' mental baggage
2. 4.1.2   The kids' roles in their "alone world"
3. 4.1.3   The parents' mental baggage
4. 4.1.4   The parents' relationship to the exes

4.1.1 THE KIDS' MENTAL BAGGAGE

Did the kids have a hard time dealing with the break-up of the parents? Are they traumatized and still affected by certain events? Do the kids have a steady and good relationship with the other parent? A stable and well-rounded parent can suddenly "lose it" if the spouse leaves him/her, especially if it's for another man/woman. Feeling numb and hurt by their painful emotions, a parent can indirectly influence the children to be on their side. The kids feel sorry for and take the responsibility for the hurting parent, while at the same time possibly distancing themselves from the parent who left them. They may even refuse to see that parent for a while. This experience can be tough for a child to handle and could weigh heavily as mental baggage for the blended family. When the fusion parent is aware of this, it will be easier to deal with otherwise inexplicable behaviour and reactions from the kids, and the fusion parent will be able to find a way to be there for them.

4.1.2 THE KIDS' ROLES IN THEIR "ALONE WORLD"

Did the parent live alone with the kids for many years? Did the kids take all the space on a daily basis? Did the kids mature quickly due to the fact that the parent lacked interaction with other adults? For example, if the parent lived alone with the kids for many years, they have created their own routines, habits, and camaraderie. Because of this, they may have a difficult time opening up to a new participant in their life. The parent, lacking adult interaction, will most likely involve the kids in their adult life. A lot of patience and understanding is required from both the parent and the fusion parent in order to change old habits and make the new blended family functional.

4.1.3 THE PARENTS' MENTAL BAGGAGE

Did the parent suffer emotionally from the break-up? Is the parent very independent and accustomed to handling everything alone? If a parent in the new blended family was hurt emotionally, they will most likely be in defense mode and have a hard time "letting go" and trusting the new partner. At the same time, they are also accustomed to handling everything and feel as though they don't need help and advice from the new partner. When the fusion parent is familiar with these emotions, then they can both work towards being able to "let go."

4.1.4 THE PARENTS' RELATIONSHIP TO THE EXES

Is it difficult for the parent for work out practical issues with their ex? Did the parent commit to arrangements with regard to birthdays, PTA meetings, and other social gatherings? Maybe the parent does not have a good relationship with the ex and is always in a battle with them, thus the parents are unable to participate together at social gatherings with the kids, and may also have difficulty taking turns when it comes to hosting birthday celebrations. The above-mentioned situation will influence the daily life of the fusion family, so it's important to be aware of the magnitude of this conflict in order to know how to deal with it. It's also good to be aware of the reason for the problems-if the parent did not inform the fusion parent about the situation, this could create unnecessary issues. It's always better to be honest when there are unpleasant issues to deal with.

Reflection

By knowing each other's background and history it's easier to understand actions and reactions related to old patterns and hurt feelings. The reciprocated openness about one's past should be dealt with in a trustworthy manner. It's important to accept the past as the past; it is a part of the baggage you both have in life. Instead of placing blame and dredging up old issues, it's better to use your history and feelings as tools by which you can plan your blended life

---

4.2 INTERVIEW WITH A FUSION FAMILY

Dianne and Michael have been dating for two and a half years. They split up at one time, but are now moving in together. Dianne has two kids: Martin, 14 years old and Emily, 11 years old. They live with Dianne and see their dad every other weekend. Michael also has two kids: Mark, 10 and Mia, 12. Michael has the kids every other weekend at his vacation home, which is fifty miles away from where Dianne and Michael live.

Q: How do you deal with the exes, the kids, and vacations?

Dianne: *I stress out just thinking about planning a vacation. I have an ex-husband and he has an ex-wife. Michael's ex-wife is also married now. The first year we were together we didn't even try to plan a vacation for the six of us. But this year we did go on vacation, all of us. If we are going on vacation next year, we better start planning soon. To make it work, I first have to get permission from work, then I ask my ex and he'll have to ask his ex; Michael will have to do the same thing with regard to his family. It's difficult, because everyone wants to go on vacation at the end of the summer.*

Q: Do you have a set schedule for when you see the kids? If so, did you have to coordinate your schedule with Michael's?

Dianne: *I have always had a set schedule right from the beginning. I haven't changed it at all, not even when it comes to Christmas. I have the kids every other Christmas. Also, with regard to vacations, we split the time between us.*

Michael: *We don't have all of the kids during the Christmas holidays, we gave that up a long time ago. So when we do not have the kids, every other year, we spend time with my family or Dianne's.*

Q: Michael, are you able to bring your kids to Dianne's family?

Michael: *I think my family would be disappointed if they didn't see the kids that year and Dianne and I don't HAVE TO spend Christmas together.*

Dianne: *But I think the kids would enjoy it, if we did. Mia likes family gatherings and all the buzz around the holidays. However, it's better to leave things the way they are.*

Q: So, you don't spend Christmas together?

Dianne: *We don't and it's not a problem.*

Michael: *My ex and I… if I have them at Christmas, then she'll have them at New Year; the following year vice versa. So the years when we don't have any kids, Dianne and I are together.*

Q: What are your considerations with regard to your living arrangements?

Michael: *It's a long story. My vacation home is in between my work place and where the kids live. The school bus stops here and when they get older, they'll take the bus themselves to my place, where they have their own rooms and things, so they feel it's their house as well.*

Dianne's kids have their own rooms here at her house and it would be difficult space-wise for my kids to have their own rooms. When we have the kids, Dianne has hers here and I have mine at the vacation home. There's a fifty mile distance between the kids' house and our apartment, and I work in different city.

Dianne: *It's not like we don't see each other.*

Michael: *Sometimes we are at the apartment and sometimes at my vacation home. We take turns sleeping on air-mattresses.*

Dianne: *In the beginning it was difficult figuring out where we should stay. It was too much planning, and I was always thinking ahead, instead of day by day. If Michael's kids lived closer, we might have considered living together, all six of us. Logistically it's difficult to figure out where we would all live together, because of the distances to the other parents' house.*

Q: Where do you celebrate the kids' birthdays?

Dianne: *Emily had her birthday in August and we were at her dad's house. All of my family was there and Michael and his kids as well. Next it's Martin's birthday and we'll have brunch here. Michael's* *sister and his parents are also invited. Martin's dad and his half-brother are invited. I have always celebrated birthdays with their dad, ever since I got divorced.*

Q: What do you do, Michael?

Michael: *I attempted celebrating birthdays with my ex and that didn't work. She has been with one of my friends for eight years now, so that's the way things are… he has an "incriminating" family, if you know what I mean. My parents don't like him either. However, I'm okay with him. I celebrate their birthdays on the weekend, when they are at my place. When they are with their mom, she celebrates it then. This way they get to celebrate their birthday twice every year.*

Dianne: *I don't do it that way. There's no correct way of doing it. I try to get a feel for what the kids want. In the beginning, right after my divorce, I couldn't stand my ex. However, my kids could, so I had to for their sake. I was thinking about why I agreed to celebrate with him and promised myself that it would be the last time I would agree to it. The following year I agreed again, because of my kids and what they wanted. But now I'm used to it. It was difficult, because he had a new girlfriend and I was single. It felt like there was an imbalance. But when I met Michael, it became more balanced again.*

Michael: *My kids were baptized two years ago and my ex and I celebrated the baptism together in a village hall. The seating plan was carefully made. Her family in the middle, my family at one end and her new family at the other end. Her family was the link between all the families. The kids were the center of all this. If Mia has her confirmation, I'm not doing this again with my ex, but Dianne and her kids are of course invited.*

Dianne: *Martin had his confirmation this year and Michael and his kids attended. It's difficult to balance the selection of whom to invite from your ex's family. I have a huge family now and he has hardly any. My ex wants to bring his other ex-wife and I want to invite Michael's family. Then my ex wanted to invite some of his friends* to balance out my numbers. But I didn't agree to have strangers attend and Martin didn't either. This resulted in that we only invited Michael, Mark, and Mia, not his entire family. When Mia has her confirmation, I don't think my entire family will attend, but we haven't discussed it yet.

Michael: *I asked Mia if her mom would throw her a big party and she said she would. My ex has a huge family just like Dianne. I told Mia that I would give her something else to choose from: a laptop, a trip abroad, or a family party with Dianne and myself. She chose the trip. Just her and I together. This way I don't have to see her mom. My parents are sad to miss out on a party, but we could take them out for dinner or make dinner for them here.*

Dianne: *There are a lot of things to account for.*

Michael: *Mia will get both a party and a trip.*

My evaluation

Dianne and Michael do not celebrate Christmas with all their children gathered together.

The advantage of this solution is that it is not so stressful as it is to many other families, where you spend a lot of energy coordinating time with the exes in order to celebrate Christmas as one family. Dianne and Michael continue their own traditions and are comfortable with them.

The disadvantage of this solution is that Dianne and Michael do not get the opportunity to introduce their own family traditions surrounding Christmas. A tradition the children could help to define and thus look forward to.

It's important to create new traditions in order to enhance the sense of community and belonging in your blended family. Traditions create a stable foundation for the children and they then know what to expect.

Michael has now decided not to participate in celebrations held for the children with his ex and her family.

The advantage of this solution is that Michael now does not have to socialize with his ex-wife and her family and hence have to assume a different role for the sake of the children. Likewise, he can now, regardless of his ex-wife's plans and arrangements, do what he wants to do for the children. He does no longer have to coordinate and agree with his ex about how an event should take place.

The sad thing about ending the joint events, is that Michael's children seemed to do fine with these events with both their mother and their father and were not affected by how their father felt about the situations.

I do not think we should underestimate the value of a joint celebration for the children and their blended families arranged by mom and dad. It tells them that both parents appear to have accepted the situation as it is and that they are ok with it.

The joint events also support the children's sense of having a 'normal' family which now has been extended with additional members.

Michael and Dianne do not live together when Michael's children are staying with him.

The advantage of this solution is that Michael can give the children his undivided attention when they stay with him. It is also more convenient when it comes to driving the children to and from school.

Similarly, Dianne has the opportunity to have alone time with her children when Michael is away.

The disadvantage of this solution is that Michael and Diane's life is very fragmented. It's difficult for them to feel like a family when they are not together very often.

When they are together, all six of them, space is limited both at the apartment and at the cottage. Therefore, it feels like visiting and not really belonging.

I think it is important for blended families to create space, rooms or areas for all of their children. If it isn't possible for every child to have his/her own room, we can create an area for the child with his/her own personal things and clothes. That makes the child feel reassured and gives him/her a sense of belonging.

4.3 TOOLS OF THE FUSION COACH: GOALS FOR YOUR FUSION FAMILY AND HOW TO REACH THEM

If you think there are too many options and not sure about which direction to choose, you can start by defining what you are aiming for in your fusion family. The goal can be something you wish to attain together as a family or something you want individually as a parent.

To function as and become a completely integrated family, just like a "nuclear" family.

The above-mentioned goal does not have clearly defined boundaries for when it has been attained. Therefore, you should ask yourselves these questions: What is the timeline for attaining this goal? How do we know when we have attained the goal or part of it?

The answers could be:

1. When the kids trust the fusion parent as well as the parent.
2. When you handle a kid's issues without considering if it's your own kid or not.
3. When the kids recognize and accept that your role as a fusion parent is equal to the parent.
4. When both the kids and the adults focus on the positive traits in one another.

5. When everyone is aware of how they can improve each other's lives.

The above exercise can be done together with the kids. For instance, you could ask them:

What we can do in order to make this a very special place for you to live?

If you have grown-up kids, ask them first. The younger kids will listen to the older kids and think about what to say when it's their turn. You may choose to write the answers down and post them where every one can see them. The kids will very likely hold you accountable for the lists and help create an honest and loving atmosphere in your home. Reflective questions to the kids regarding their needs and wishes are of great importance, especially in blended families where it may be difficult for a child to identify your role and status in the new family constellation.

If you are a planner, who likes lists and has the need to define your goals, you will most likely encounter the following questions:

1. What is needed in order to attain the goal?
2. Why do we want to attain this goal?
3. How do we get there?

I would recommend that you make a what-why-how to-plan. The plan can be based on the goal itself and/or partial goals.

The What: The result, including the goal and/or partial goal.
The Why: The reason, why you want that result. This should include the motivating factors.
The How to: Your defined plan of action. What is needed to reach the goal?

It could look something like this:
What: We want to function like a fully integrated family within a two year time frame. Next, write down why you want to attain this goal and what the motivation is for achieving it.

Why: Why is it important to us, what do we gain, what's the real reason for this and how are we going to feel when we reach this goal?

How to: What is our specific plan to attain this, what do we need to get to the result, what can we do starting today?

If this seems a little overwhelming, start by prioritizing the issues and focus on the most important one right now. Sometimes it's the little things that make a huge difference.

5. PLANNING YOUR BLENDED LIFE: IS IT REALLY NECESSARY?

The answer is: Yes! The most important milestone to reach is matching each other's expectations and demands in order to create the foundation of a well-balanced and functional family. Try asking each other: What do you expect of me with regard to your kids? Start an open dialogue about what you expect, demand, and hope for in each other, making sure to include the not-so-pleasant, emotional, and practical aspects.

The questionnaire below is based on my own family situation. The clarification of and consensus to the issues will eliminate the number of discussions you may have in your fusion family. The importance of these questions will be discussed later on in the book.

I have created the following list of questions and think it's important that both you and your partner know the answers to them:

1. Are you willing to take responsibility for my kids the same way you do towards your own?
2. Will you actively participate in the upbringing of my kids?

3. Will you prioritize my kids the same way you prioritize your own?
4. Will you solve my kids' problems in everyday life?
5. Will you care for my kids when they are sick?
6. What is your attitude towards my ex?
7. How do we handle socializing with my ex?
8. Will you participate in social gatherings with regard to school?
9. Will you participate in activities if my ex is participating as well?
10. Will you drive my kids to their appointments?

5.1 RULES FOR THE BLENDED LIFE TOGETHER

You and your partner will both be carrying baggage that doesn't exist in a "nuclear" family. For example: your relationship with your ex, hurt feelings, jealousy, scheduling/planning, child support, upbringing of the kids, habits, traditions, etc. The odds of a blended family succeeding are bad because of this baggage. You don't start out with a clean slate. I have heard this many times, "It will all work out because we love each other." During the first year, you might have the extra energy in dealing with your hurt feelings, hiding your disappointment and letting things go easily, until the day comes when you can't hold back any longer. By defining a set of rules with regard to the baggage you both carry, you will find yourselves on a straight path.

Below are my suggestions of important rules. Posting these on the fridge is recommended.

1. **Support each other's new role as a fusion parent.**

It's important to let the kids know that the fusion parent has the same authority in the blended family as the biological parent. Let the fusion parent handle situations and support them if problems occur.

2. **Define for the kids how they are to behave towards the fusion parent. It's important to let the kids know that ignoring the fusion parent is not acceptable.**

In the beginning, because you are careful in your new role as a fusion parent, you may find yourself being ignored by the kids. You feel you should react to it, but you don't reprimand the kids. In this situation, it's important that the parent reprimands the kids and explains to them why the behaviour is unacceptable. Both rules are important because they set the parameters for acceptable behaviour, which then creates a feeling a security for the kids. The responsibility of enforcing the rules belongs to the parents.

3. **Show affection to each other on a daily basis, even if you are busy with the kids.**

It's a big job becoming a fusion parent. You will spend a lot of mental energy trying to do everything right for the kids. You may also "forget'" about each other when the kids are present. It's important to show affection towards your partner in order to handle conflicts better – affection has a positive influence on your mental energy. This will enable you to feel more resourceful in case of a conflict or problem.

4. **Don't ask questions about your partner's ex if you can't handle the answer.**

Example: My girlfriend Kate couldn't resist asking her new partner about his ex-wife. He answered truthfully saying, "She is very beautiful." Kate didn't stop at that and continued, "What's her figure like?" The answer she got was, "She is what I would call an ideal woman." Kate's new partner thought these questions were based on curiosity, but here is what Kate heard:

He said: "She is very beautiful."
She heard: Too bad I have to settle with you. I'd rather have my ex back.

He said: "She is what I would call an ideal woman."

She heard: I love ideal women. But you are not ideal, so I have to settle for less. If you love me, then do something about it so you will become more like my ideal. I can't stand having to settle with a less perfect body like yours.

Kate's self-worth took a dive due to this conversation and a lot of time passed before it got restored. I asked her if she shared with him what was going on with her emotionally, and she replied that she was too embarrassed to do so. She could just have asked for a compliment if she needed one, but instead she dug deeper. Conclusion: Drop the painful questions about the ex.

5. **Don't look for affirmation of yourself by criticizing your partner's ex.**

For the fusion parent it's important not to look for affirmation and affection by criticizing your partner's ex. Your partner chose their ex at one point in time, and should not be held accountable. The decision took place in the past, which is not important for the present.

6. **Speak kindly of your partner's kids despite being angry.**
7. **Don't accuse each other of inadequacy when it comes to the upbringing of the kids.**

It's inevitable that you will feel frustration with regard to your fusion kids. If this is an ongoing occurrence, you need to bring it up with your partner. Make sure you speak in a non-accusatory manner and stay calm during the conversation with your partner.

8. **Remember to appreciate one another in your new roles as fusion parents.**

It's good for your self-esteem when your partner notices and appreciates your actions towards their kids. This then strengthens your courage and willingness in continuing to work actively toward a loving relationship with the fusion kids.

9. **Set time aside to discuss daily matters.**

This rule is important especially in the beginning of your relationship when you might feel a little insecure. Be honest with each other and discuss daily situations and/or conflicts you had with the kids. Describe the experiences and emotions you encountered.

10. **Mutually praise each other's kids when they deserve it.**

When you reciprocate praising the kids, you will strengthen your trust in the fusion parent's love and best intentions for your own kids. When you are good at praising each other's kids, then it becomes easier for the parent to accept those situations when the fusion parent must reprimand their partners' kids.

It can be difficult to always comply by the above-mentioned rules. However, they can be very helpful when something goes wrong and you need to understand the reason it happened. The lack of compliance by any or some of the rules can create feelings of hurtfulness, sadness, jealousy, and anger.

5.2 FINDING THE COMMON THREAD IN ATTITUDES, HABITS, AND UPBRINGING

In a blended family it's important that the adults work towards the kids perceiving them as a single unit. It's paramount to define the most fundamental values of the family, such as the upbringing and well being of the kids. It's difficult to function well in a family where only one parent has kids, if the fusion parent without kids does not want to be actively involved. This situation will result in frustration for both parents. The parent needs to demand participation of the fusion parent in all aspects of the kids' well being. Even if you don't agree with their opinion on different aspects, do listen and be open-minded. Hopefully this will result in some sort of compromise as to what is best for the blended family, and for the family to thrive and be functional.

The goal of finding a common thread is integrates both the parents and the kids in the family. The kids should be confident knowing that whether they question the parent or the fusion parent, the answer will be the same. This way the kids can rely on the fusion parent to be there for them and they won't always need the parent when they have issues.

My own story

Here is a cute little example of what you can gain when you stand united as parents: After Jegwan and I moved in together in our new house, Thursday/Allowance/Payday came along. Jegwan wasn't home yet. My boys came to me asking for their allowance. His kids, Oscar and Andrea, stood in the background quietly looking on and then went into their room. I handed my boys their allowance and then went into both Andrea and Oscar's rooms asking them about the amount of their allowances. "Here you go," I said, handing them the amount they told me they received each week. They both were genuinely happy and thanked me many times, as if I had done something special for them. I realized that they felt they couldn't ask ME for their allowance and thought they would have to wait until their dad came home.

I felt warm in my heart due to their reaction, and decided that when next Allowance Day came around I would do the same thing. It was a small gesture on my behalf, however my actions showed Andrea and Oscar that I care for them the same way I care for my own boys.

> **Reflection**
> If you make an effort to agree upon solutions for the important issues regarding the kids, then you make it easier for the kids. They will no longer have to try to figure out the practical issues. This will make everyday life less problematic.

5.3 CHECKLIST FOR THE PRACTICAL PART OF BLENDED LIFE – ARE WE IN CONTROL?

I am sure a lot of you have experienced the differences in opinion when it comes to disciplining, bed times, table manners, food preferences, TV and computer rules, habits, traditions, holidays, birthdays, hobbies, clothing, allowances, etc. The kids in a blended family expect things to be done the same way, at the same time, in the same order as they were used to before they entered the blended family.

You can imagine how much kids may object if things are done the "wrong way" – that is, not the way they are used to. Therefore, it's a good idea to prepare the kids for all the adjustments and changes that are going to be different from those to which they'd become accustomed. When the adults have defined the new rules/routines, they can then jointly explain them to the kids.

I have created a list of issues that are important to clarify with each other, as you may have different habit and/or rules for your own kids. The relevance of the ideas below depends on the relationship you have with your kids.

Issues	Example of possible discrepancies
Baths/hair washing	Some kids take a bath and have their hair washed every day and others may only do this 2-3 times a week.
Table manners	Some kids eat faster then others. Are they supposed to wait until every one has food on their plate before they start eating or do they start eating when they are ready? Do they have to wait until everyone is done before leaving the table? Is dinner time for conversation or do they eat quietly? Are they supposed help clear the table?

Saving accounts	Some kids have one, others don't.
TV/Computer/ Video Games	Some kids are allowed to play as much as they want, others only for certain amounts of time per day.
Materialism	Some kids receive everything they ask for, others have to save up and use their allowance if they want a new toy.
Sports	Some kids participate in sports and are dropped off and picked up, others aren't allowed until they can drive themselves to the events. How many sports and how often?
Birthdays	Special birthday traditions? Does the whole family of the child participate including the ex's family or are there two separate birthday celebrations? How much is spent on presents?
Packing for Holidays/ Vacations	Some kids pack their own bag; others have their parents pack for them.
Having friends over	Some kids can freely see their friends and don't have to ask permission, others have to ask and aren't allowed to see friends very often.
Curfews	What time do kids have to be home in the evening? Some kids stay out until darkness falls, others have a set time.
Homework	Some kids have to do homework right after they come home from school; others are allowed to play first. Some get help with homework, others have to figure it out themselves.

Allowance	When and how much? Do they receive an allowance without any chores or do they do chores in order to receive an allowance? Are they free to spend it in any manner they choose or are there limitations?
Food	What are rules for "eating your veggies" and "try it before you say you don't like it"? Do we make different menus? What are the kids allowed to drink with their meals: milk, water, juice, or sodas? Some kids are supposed to ask for food, others help themselves.
School lunches	What is usually packed? What is preferred? For example, whole wheat or white bread sandwiches?
Breakfast	What is served? Fruit Loops vs. oatmeal?
Bedclothes	On weekends are the kids allowed to wear their pyjamas all day or do they have to get dressed as soon as they get up?
Cleaning up	Some kids are taught to clean up; some have it done for them by the parents.
Chores	How many and what are they?
Bedtime	Despite being the same age, some kids can stay up later than others. If the kids are older, are they allowed to stay up as long as the parents?
To cater or not to cater	Do you respond to every request made by your kid or are they self-sufficient?

Clothing	Some kids have to wear clean clothes every day, others will wear the same pair of jeans for a couple of days. Some kids decide themselves what to wear while others don't have the choice.
Candy and sodas	How much and how often?
Bedtime routines	Some kids are used to stories and the parent lying down with them until they are asleep, others get a hug and kiss and fall asleep on their own.
Clothes purchasing	Some parents shop at discount stores and some only buy brand names.

Tabel 1: Example of possible discrepancies

5.4   TAKING RESPONSIBILITY

5.4.1   "JUST-WAIT-TILL-DADDY-COMES-HOME"

As I mentioned earlier, if you want your blended family to succeed, it's a necessity that both of you take responsibility for all the kids, regardless of whether you are a parent or not. The amount of effort you put in depends on the ages of the kids. Again, if you choose the solution "I parent my kids, you parent yours" you will inevitably experience a situation with the fusion kid that you can't handle in the way you would handle with your own kid. You will have to wait until the parent is present, so they can handle it. This may make you look like a "Just-wait-till-daddy-comes-home" person, which is respectful neither towards yourself, your partner, nor the kids.

If you handle the situation with the fusion kids yourself, you won't feel like a tattletale and can then inform your partner of what happened and how you handled it. At the same time, it's important that the kids feel secure and know they won't get reprimanded twice, and feel good that the fusion parent handled the situation. There is no reason for the parent to handle a situation they wasn't involved in. Since expectations of the kids can vary from kid to kid, choosing the "I parent my kids, you parent yours" solution can create discord between the parent and the fusion parent. This solution could also create feelings of inadequacy as a parent, when trying to act on the kids behavior on behalf of the fusion parent.

Because your expectations for the kids might vary from your partner's, you might find yourself pointing fingers at each other for bad parenting. The parent is not directly responsible for ALL the demands of the kids. The pressure that is put on the parent does not create a solid ground for a healthy and mutually beneficial relationship, since the parent will feel monitored, measured, and weighed. In connection with "telling on" each other's kids, I recommend that you read section <u>5.7.3 Pitfall 3: Being tense and pressuring your kids</u>

> **Reflection**
> The parent needs the reassurance of knowing that the fusion parent takes responsibility for situations where their limits are exceeded instead of passively waiting for the parent's efforts.
>
> It gives the parent inner peace and reassurance since they don't have to constantly observe the kids on behalf of the fusion parent. The fusion parents must know for themselves that situations with children are addressed in proper and orderly manners.

5.5 INTERVIEW WITH A FUSION FAMILY

Thomas lives with Anne and Anne's daughter Eline, who is three and a half years old. They have lived together for a half year.

Questions to Thomas:

Q: What were your expectations and/or requirements for Anne in your role as a fusion dad?

Answer: *I very much wanted to be allowed to enter on equal terms. I, just as much as Anne, was allowed to participate in and influence the upbringing of Eline. It was actually very important for me not to feel that I had been left on the sidelines, but instead I was equal with Anne. It would be strange to live with Anne, and especially Eline, and not have any influence on her upbringing. It was important for me to feel included in order to not feel disregarded and unimportant. Eline would probably not respect me as much if I did not take part in solving problems along the way.*

Q: How would you handle a situation where Eline crosses your line, but not Anne's?

Answer: *When my line is crossed, I will discipline her. Anne will have to back me up, whether she agrees or not. Anne often adds this to the situation, "You must listen to what Thomas says." We discuss it afterwards and Anne sometimes suggests to me that I could also do such and such, and if she has experience or an alternative idea she shares it with me. If it is me who is face to face with Eline, I have the right to decide and Anne does not overrule that. Sometimes Eline crosses the line and Anne does not respond, and I feel she ought to say something.*

Anne comments: *Sometimes I go in and protect Thomas' limits, since I often have much wider limits than he has. I have helped Thomas in situations where he has a conflict with Eline. Thomas asked me to immediately stop this, because he said I deprived him of his authority. I wanted to protect Thomas and just thought I had the right solution for how the situation could have been resolved.*

Q: How would you handle a situation where you did not agree with Anne's way of disciplining Eline?

Answer: *It hasn't happened very often. We have been lucky in the sense that we have fairly similar outlooks on how children should be disciplined. Of course, there may be disagreements from time to time, where I must state that I do not agree. But we only discuss it when Eline isn't present, so that she does not perceive this as a disagreement between the two of us. We discuss the situation and our different opinions. I must add that Anne has great educational insight, so I often realize that Anne is right. Anne also has the most experience with Eline and knows what works and what does not work in different situations. Most of the time I respect what Anne says but comment on it occasionally afterwards.*

Q: How do you and Anne handle the practical things with regard to Eline?

Answer: *We actually have not discussed it yet. Since I want to be equal to Anne, I will have to take responsibility the same way she does. However, it's mostly Anne who handles the practical stuff. If Anne has an appointment, I pick Eline up, but usually it happens only if Anne can't make it. However, for a long time I was the only one reading bedtime stories for Eline. Later on Anne and I took turns reading, but then Eline insisted that it should only be her mother who read to her. Anne and I talked a little about whether we should stick to the principle that we take turns to read, or if it was okay that Eline only wanted her mother to read to her. We ended up letting Eline decide. I always put a little drawing in Eline's lunchbox. This was actually Anne's idea and I have so far created a bit more imaginative drawings than Anne's stick figures. So for the longest time Eline did not want Anne's drawings, because my drawings were funnier.*

My evaluation
Thomas has always demanded that he participate in the upbringing of Eline on the same level as Anne.

The advantage of this solution is that Thomas can act freely and let Eline know if she is 'out of line'. He does not have to ask

Anne to take care of it, but can handle situations as they occur. Anne no longer needs to do the disciplining all the time.

Eline will with this solution also know Thomas' role in her life and that his words also count equally to those of her mother. This role will be supported when Anne backs him up in front of Eline and demands that she listens to him.

However, it is important for a fusion parent's authority that he/she handles the conflict with the child without the parent's involvement. Form and content can always be discussed afterward if the parent did not agree.

For some children it may take a long time before they fully accept the fusion parent's role in regards to discipline. They already have a parent who disciplines them, however, if the parent constantly stresses that the fusion parent has his/her full support in disciplining them, the children will usually accept it sooner than later.

If I have to mention an immediate disadvantage of this solution, it may be that Thomas initially has difficulties feeling authentic in his role towards Eline. And that he is not comfortable having to correct her. Therefore, he might spend too much energy and pay too much attention to Eline's behavior, in order to manifest his new role, both towards himself, but also towards Anne and Eline. He does not posses that role naturally like Anne does, he has to create it, and can only do so through actions.

It is important for me to point out, that whether you yourself are a parent or not, it may take some time and considerable self-insight to feel completely authentic in your role as the disciplinarian towards your fusion children. Be honest and ask yourself, why it is important to you in this situation to discipline the children. You might be amazed by the response that could be something like: "Let me get rid of my uncertainty as a fusion parent as soon as possible. I can only get rid of it by being very uptight with the kids." Perhaps it might be a good idea to wait until there's something important, before you discipline or correct them.

5.6 TOOLS OF THE FUSION COACH: VALUE CLARIFICATION

In this section I have written about rules and the importance of finding common ground. After reading this, if you still feel, "We are too different, this isn't going to work", I recommend that you take a look your values. When I use the word value in this context, it should be interpreted as a feeling. You can try to handle your differences as follows:

You and your partner ask yourselves: What is important to me in our relationship?

Make a list of your individual values, and then prioritize the items on your list.

Afterwards you use a scale from 1-10, 10 being the highest. Assess how fulfilled these values are in your relationship right now.

Maybe your partner has "freedom" on the top of the list and maybe you have "security" on the top of yours. Both of you have assessed your values to a "three", but want it to be a "ten".

You can then ask yourself: What do I have to do to feel more secure?

Your partner asks him/herself: What do I have to do to feel more freedom?

This exercise will make you aware of yours and partner's values. This can be a very important insight to have and help you to realize that you come from two different places. For instance: When your partner fulfils their desire for freedom, you might easily feel uncomfortable and perceive it as a lack of interest in you if they choose to do things alone.

When your most important values are mapped out, you immediately create a better understanding of each other's actions and reactions. Example: Next time your partner chooses to go sailing, you may feel more calm and think they are simply fulfilling their need for freedom, and it has nothing to do with you.

On the basis of individual values, you can now create common values for your relationship. You do this by strengthening the values you have in common.

5.7 HOW TO AVOID THE 10 WORST PITFALLS OF THE FUSION FAMILY

There are many pitfalls for the fusion family. In this section I have tried to describe and raise awareness of the most common pitfalls, including suggestions as how to avoid them. If you do encounter a pitfall after reading this, you will know what went wrong and hopefully will get back on track faster.

5.7.1 PITFALL 1: THE RELATIONSHIP TO THE EX

From the very beginning, we have to face the fact that the ex will be a part of our life as a fusion family. Although this can be incredibly difficult, we have to accept the importance of the role the ex plays in our children's lives. The ex is part of the baggage the blended family is forced to accept and everyone must try to work with them.

The relationship to the ex has an even more important role when you are in a blended family.

Besides taking care of your blended family's problems, you also have to deal with the problems of the ex or exes. The intensity of fighting with the ex must never become so pervasive that the family suffers. Kids will quickly understand there is trouble between mother and father, even though they have not heard or seen anything in particular. It is important to remember that engaging in too many battles with the ex can seriously harm the kids. Make sure you pick your battles wisely. Only choose battles that are important for the well-being of the kids. Define your limitations and stick with them.

It is easy for the adults in the blended family to make the ex the scapegoat – in doing so, you may feel more connected to one another. Be careful not to let things get out of context. Don't let your emotions rule; instead, use rational thinking in a conflict with the ex. Also keep in mind that it can be tempting for us as a fusion parent to look for "evidence" for our partners love for us, by criticizing their ex. Remember that jealousy impairs your judgment of the situation with the ex. It's a good idea to think rationally about whether or not to start arguing about the ex.

Finances are often a factor for arguments in the blended family. Child support, and at times alimony, must be paid year after year. This issue is very likely a nuisance, both financially and emotionally, to the blended family.

There are many aspects of the financial ties/agreements you have with the ex.

In the United States there is no fixed amount for child support, it is based on the income of both parents and is different from state to state. Alimony is based solely on the judge's discretion and decision and is not a mathematical equation. On the webpage: http://divorce.lovetoknow.com/Main_Page you can calculate, by state, the amount you will have to pay.

The amount might be determined by the court and is therefore not to be changed, but it's a part of the baggage that the fusion parent is forced to accept.

Agreements, other than those just mentioned, could be tied to strong emotions. I have chosen to deal with the issues from the perspectives of the partner, the fusion parent, and the kids.

You might have agreed to pay a great amount of child support because you felt guilty about the divorce and wanted to settle for peace of mind. All of a sudden, your partner confronts you about this and have to justify your reasoning. The fusion parent demands that you explain why the ex should receive so much money. You explain it by saying, that the ex is in a tough financial situation and they are the parent of the kids, and that's why you agreed to the amount in the past. However, if the fusion parent is right by arguing that the agreement is unreasonable and CAN be altered, then you should try to reach a more fair deal with the ex.

As a fusion parent, you might feel bitter and complain about the lifestyle of your partner's ex, whose lifestyle seems extravagant at the expense of your partner while you are in a tough financial situation because of them.

If your partner agrees to discuss the financial situation with their ex, they are showing responsibility for your fusion family's finances and making them a priority. It also shows that your finances are more important than those of the ex. On the other hand, if agreements cannot be altered, you will have to accept them as a part of the baggage of your partner's life.

Regardless of the financial agreements with the ex, I think it's important to the kids that you as a team don't continually argue about money and deals you have made with the ex. It's wise to, at times, just experience the joy of buying something for them yourself. To the kids this shows that you care for them. It's not about materialism to them and it's our responsibility as parents to provide for our kids the way they expect us to provide for them. Do not let feelings of revenge towards the ex get in the way of kids' right to feel safe and secure. It's important for them to know that they are cared for no matter where they are.

Discuss financial issues later on, if necessary. Remember, let yourself be the happy giving person to happy receiving kids once in a while.

5.7.2 PITFALL 2: THE KIDS' ROLES IN THE BLENDED FAMILY, BUT WHAT ABOUT ME?

The kids' roles were different when you were alone with them or still together with your ex. The roles have changed because the kids are now a part of the blended family. The roles could be part of the baggage you carry, and it'll take time, understanding, and patience to change old habits.

Regardless of whether the fusion parent has any kids, the kids' roles are difficult to deal with for both of you. You might discover aspects of your kids' behavior you didn't know could cause trouble or problems. But when the fusion parent points out issues, the parent automatically defends their kids' behavior. And although the parent may agree with the perspective of the fusion parent, they may side one way or the other with regard to the kids' behavior in order to prove the fusion parent right or wrong.

It takes a lot of courage for a parent to admit to the fusion parent that they need to make changes with regard to certain issues with the kids in order for everyone to live together peacefully. The fusion parent must therefore make every effort to be worthy of the parent's trust by welcoming and constructively contributing suggestions for how to change things.

The parent and the fusion parent must define the kids' new roles jointly. While this isn't easy, it is necessary to agree about the following:

1. How much "space" do we give the kids?
2. How much attention is reasonable for kids to demand of adults?
3. What's reasonable with regard to kids demanding full attention from the parent, leaving no room for the fusion parent?
4. Is it reasonable for the parent to ask the kids for alone time with the fusion parent?

When you initiate the conversation/discussion on the above issues, it is important that it's based first on your own needs and secondly on children's needs. The reason for this selfish priority is that you cannot be both fully present and feel empathy towards others if you consistently feel deprived on a daily basis. Be honest about your need for time with each other, and also about your need for time with the children. Your partner might have the need to spend a lot of time with the kids, while you prefer a nice balance of time spent with both.

One should try to find a reasonable balance that meets the needs of adult time with each other and the children's need of time with their parents. If such a balance can be created, you will feel greater inner happiness and satisfaction, and therefore have more energy for the children. A simple but effective way for adult partners to recharge is to spend 20-30 minutes together when they get home from work, embracing and giving full attention to one another.

> **Reflection**
> By first giving time to each other you can then give full attention to the children, attention that comes from a warm and loving heart. If, however, you consistently set yourself aside for sake of the kids, you can very easily end up feeling like a martyr: "All I have had to sacrifice for the children's sake" or "I've done everything for the children and this is all I get in return." The risk is that you may feel belittled, unfairly treated, and neglected. It is therefore important that both partners are honest about their need for time with each other and with the children, even though deep inside they may feel selfish. It is better to express this need and together try to find a compromise so that one party is not consistently deprived. Your partner may actually feel surprised and a little flattered by knowing that their presence was missed.

5.7.3   PITFALL 3: BEING TENSE AND PRESSURING YOUR KIDS

Whether you admit it or not, it's incredibly hard not to always be tense and to constantly try to stay abreast of situations which may cast doubt on how you and others perceive your children. When this happens, how can you for example:

- Predict the outcome of a given situation and be prepared
- Prevent your children from crossing the line
- Ensure that the children give a hug to fusion parent when expected

- Ensure that the children look forward to the fusions parent's proposed activity
- Ensure that the children notice when the fusion parent does something nice

The examples are countless, and I think we all have felt these emotions to a greater or lesser extent. Why this excruciating "performance anxiety" on behalf of our children? It may be because we are basically afraid that the fusion parent will perceive our children as burdensome, unthankful, and not well behaved, although we know that it is not true.

As parents, we live in the fear of the fusion parent not noticing all the amazing and charming traits of our children, but instead only take note of the less fortunate ones, which they also do have. Therefore we begin to pressure our children to do and say things in certain ways that we believe clarify and highlight the positive sides of their personality. But this lasts only until the next time, when performance anxiety emerges and it starts all over again.

Here is one of the major differences between a nuclear family and a blended family: We would never ever feel this pressure regarding performance anxiety towards the biological parent of our children; neither would we feel anxiety and worry about whether the other parent is able to see the quality of our children. When you feel this pressure sneaking up on you, try to stop a moment and ask yourself whether you want to respond to it or not. If you always try to anticipate a bad situation, you risk achieving the exact opposite of what you intended.

Here's an example:
Yvonne and Curt are married and have two children each. Yvonne complains about Curt's children, which obviously makes him sad. As a consequence of this is he is very tense and anxious to prove the opposite to her – that his children are lovable and not annoying.

Ten minutes before Yvonne comes home from work, Curt is already at home with the children and is stressed out, looking at the clock. He runs to the children and says:

"Kids, Yvonne comes home in a little while. Don't forget to give her a huge hug, and also remember to say thank you for the delicious lunch she made for you yesterday. By the way, did you remember to put the empty lunchboxes in the kitchen?

Yvonne has had a tough day; don't bother her with all sorts of issues when she comes in the door! Remember to allow her to unwind. She needs that. Also remember to not take food from the refrigerator without asking first; otherwise she will just get mad at you again. Can you try to remember the rules, so she will not be so annoyed with you?"

The door opens and Yvonne enters. The children run towards her and give her a hug, thanking her nicely for the lunches, just like their father had asked of them. Curt is in the background feeling proud and happy while he awaits Yvonne's positive response, which of course will be the result of his exhortations. Now she can see how nice and loving his children are.

History repeats itself, and each time Yvonne complains about the children, Curt's desire to stay ahead and pressure the children intensifies. This continues until the day Curt feels that the children have become insecure and nervous in their relationship with Yvonne. Then it dawns on him that he knows that his pressuring has completely alienated Yvonne with regard to his children. He has made her the "scapegoat" or something "dangerous", something you should pay special attention to, something you must take into account. It was not his intention. On the contrary, he thought that he helped the children and Yvonne come together.

> **Reflection**
> Forget about pressuring the kids and let them respond freely and naturally, letting things and situations occur naturally. Do not take responsibility for the fusions parent's expected reaction and feelings. Do not try to anticipate them either. The fusion parent is responsible for their reaction in the various situations encountered.

It is recommended that you read the following section:
7.3   How to reprimand each other's kids and how to have confidence in your partner when they reprimand your kids

5.7.4   PITFALL 4: WHEN "WEEKEND KIDS" COME INTO THE NEWLY EXISTING FAMILY

It can be difficult to operate as an integrated and blended family when you only have one set of children every other weekend. When the children arrive Friday afternoon, they must first become acclimatized from the other parent's house and then find their place in the blended family.

The children coming into the existing family need to observe and discover what is happening and where they fit in. This situation can be very difficult to deal with, both for the fusion parent and the biological parent, as both parties inevitably feel that they must do everything so the kids feel welcome and wanted. The parents may have high expectations of themselves with regard to everything they'd like to do with the kids – all the attention and love they want to give them before the kids have to leave again.

Similarly, parents can very quickly feel bad for the children who have been there all the time, if the continuation of an ongoing project with them is postponed in favor of time with the weekend children. The children might feel irritated: "Oh no, the weekend the kids are here now and I have not finished my project with mom/dad." The parents need to know that they have done everything possible for the weekend kids in the relatively short time they were there, and that they have given the kids their love and affection.

In the above situation, there are many kinds of emotions and considerations involved:

1. The weekend children's need to be acclimated and settle in
2. The weekend children's need for love and care from the parent and his/her partner
3. The children's irritation with the weekend children's disruptive arrival
4. The parents need to give the weekend kids love and affection
5. The parent and his/her partner's guilty conscience towards the other children, because they need to focus on the weekend kids

These emotions must all be dealt with within a very short time so the parents do not end up feeling that it did not go as they had hoped and therefore feel inadequate. Below I have tried to give ideas on how to make it easier for all parties.

The parents can turn the arrival into something pleasant and gratifying for the whole family: "Soon A and B will arrive, and then I'll make some snacks so we can sit together and enjoy each other's company." If possible, try to create a new tradition/habit so that the kids can happily look forward to their arrival. This will give children a positive attitude towards the arrival of the weekend children; something positive happens and they feel included.

The less contact you have with your children, the harder it may be to connect with them before they have to leave again. Therefore, it's a good idea to have regular contact with them during the week, so you know before they arrive what they have experienced since you last saw them. You can create a good rapport by writing and calling your children regularly. If the children are older and have Internet access, there are plenty of opportunities to "chat" and maybe even "see" each other through a web-camera, in between the physical contact. This gives the children a sense of comfort knowing that at 7:30p.m., they will chat and/or speak with you. They also will then have the opportunity to think and prepare what they want to tell you about and what they may need help with, while you also show that you think of and care about them, even though you are not together physically.

It is obviously important to find a good and appropriate time for this contact so it does not disrupt the children's lives with the other parents. It also provides the parent and the fusion parent the opportunity to continue an ongoing dialogue about topics they have had with the children. Parents should not have to completely start from scratch trying to find out what has happened in their children's lives since they saw them last. They are already informed, and thus have the opportunity to ask about different things they have spoken or written about with the children.

To minimize possible irritation from the kids towards the weekend kids, the parents can schedule the long-term and time-consuming projects with the kids for another time when the weekend kids are not there. It is important that you do not suspend smaller projects with the children while the weekend kids are there. The children will notice if you reject them in favor of helping the weekend kids, so it is a good idea to plan in advance for this situation.

A good way to get the weekend kids to feel like a part of your blended family is to give them projects that they can continue to work on from one weekend to the next. When the weekend kids are about to come over, they now think: "I can continue building my model airplane/finish my painting." This gives them a delightful sense of belonging.

Let me give you some ideas for good projects for the weekend children:

- Puzzles of different difficulties depending on the age of the children
- Model airplane/cars

- Painting on a easel
- Lego
- Books/audiobooks from the library
- Sewing gift items for family members
- Quilting (My fusion daughter Andrea showed me how to quilt)
- Strategy games or other games that takes days to complete
- Create things out of wood, eg. a sword, shield
- Write a book or a subject of interest to the child
- Renovate property, if the children are older

It is of course necessary that the weekend children pack and bring their clothes. When I pack a bag, it is because I'm going to visit somewhere. This is also the feeling I get when I see children with their packed bags… they are going to be visiting the other parent. The hope in this situation must be that children get the feeling that when they go to stay with their mom/dad, it is also their home or at least a place where they belong. It is both practical and good for the children that they have clothes they can leave with the other parent that they don't need to drag back and forth every time. The feeling that they can take clothes out of a drawer, instead of having to take out of a bag, is of great importance for the children's sense of belonging.

The following sections, as described in this book, can also be used when weekend children are integrated into the blended family:

6.1.1 Gift 1: Creating traditions in the blended family
6.1.2 Gift 2: Making ordinary things important
6.1.3 Gift 3: A fusion parent can find his/her own niche
6.1.4 Gift 4: Doing something special with the fusion child

If you introduce some of the ideas described here, the weekend children will be able to feel like part of the blended family, and the risk of the parent and fusion parent feeling guilty when the weekend children leave is substantially minimized.

5.7.5 PITFALL 5: YOU'RE NOT MY MOM/DAD!

The above statement is likely recognizable by many fusion parents who have disciplined their fusion child. "You're not my mom/dad, so you can't tell me what do to." This statement is both expected and understandable, but it can also instigate an extreme reaction from a fusion parent: "What a brat, how dare he/she say that to me." But if you think about it for a moment, it is also an indication that the children do not know exactly what your role is in relation to them. They have already a mother and a father who discipline them. When children say something like that, you have an opportunity to then identify and explain what your role is.

My own story
Jegwan was the first of us who had to answer when my eldest son made the above statement. Jegwan replied as follows: "No. It is true, I'm not your father. But when you're here with your mother and me, we both discipline you."

You should expect that the phrase "You're not my mom/dad" will be repeated, but in different variations, at the beginning of your blended life. At this time, it is important that you give the children the same message every single time without showing anger. You may discover that the children just want to see if you've changed your mind and this time say something different.

If the children are young they will probably ask their mom/dad if it is indeed true that the fusion parent has control over them. When you as a fusion parent are consistent with your response, the children will eventually accept your response as being valid.

> **Reflection**
> Both parties in the relationship must be mutually supportive and firm towards their own children, letting them know that the new fusion parent has their full support and the authority to make decisions.

If you as a fusion parent suddenly feel that your fusion children keep you at a distance or they are reserved and hard to deal with, it may be because they feel conflicted in their loyalties.

The children may think that the other parent will be upset if they show too much joy or talk too enthusiastically about their fusion parents. Children are afraid that the "real" parent may start to believe that they prefer the fusion parent over them. They feel they cannot choose both fusion parent and the "real" parent at the same time, but that instead they face an either/or choice, which in the children's eyes can only result in denying the fusion parent.

If the fusion child repeatedly says they miss their mom/dad or consistently highlights all that the "real" parents are really good at, it is the fusion parent's responsibility to applaud and praise everything that the children say about the "real" parent and ask additional positive questions. Children will instinctively test you, the fusion parent, to see if you fully accept the "real" parent's role in their life. You may handle the situation as described by telling them "I understand that you are proud of and love your mom/dad, and I have no problem with that."

It is important as a fusion parent to not feel belittled in this situation. Even though the children praise the "real" parent, they are not simultaneously saying that you are worthless. Do not think that the children say things "between the lines" because they don't. The fusion parent should not give children this sort of scheming adult characteristic. Instead, take their words at face value, respond with care and common sense, and give the children what they ask for: your acceptance of the "real" parent.

The above situation should also apply in the reverse. The "real" parent must also assure the children that they understand that the children are happy with their fusion parents; the "real" parent should not feel less appreciated and/or unwanted if children mention the fusion parent in glowing terms.

In the beginning of my own blended family life, I could clearly feel that Andrea felt conflicted about her loyalty to her mother. She had started to like me and I do not think she felt she was allowed to. She felt that she failed her mother by preferring my way of doing something or to agree with my approach to situations that were different from her mother's way. Maybe she felt she had to choose between us and that she could not like both her mother and me equally.

She was comparing us and the resulted was that she praised her mother to me, and highlighted all the things her mother was good at. I made sure that I agreed with her and telling that she's right about her mother and I told her I understood that she was proud of her mother. Through a long period I showed Andrea my appreciation of her mother and finally it ended.

She had no further need to be assured that "I knew my role" as a fusion mom and that I accepted and recognized her mother in her life.

To this day she takes the best from her mother and me. She knows where and when to involve me and when to involve her mother. I'm better at girly stuff like hair and makeup, I think it is fun. Her mother is great at making things by hand, which I would never attempt.

When the children feel that both sets of parents accept each other's roles in their lives, loyalty conflict will eventually disappear and the children will be able to react and speak freely to both the fusion parent and the "real" parent. Most likely they will soon see the advantage of having two sets of adults to choose from. Who and what do I prefer in a given situation? Who will be the best adult to involve in a certain situation?

5.7.6 PITFALL 6: DO THE KIDS HAVE ONE OR TWO FAMILIES?

When you live together in a nuclear family, the definition of it is not something you wonder about. The parents implicitly define it as a single unit with links to both the mother and the father's families. When the children no longer live with the other parent, but are instead in a blended family, the definition of the family is no longer as clear and easily defined.

The parent who is now part of the blended family might suggest that the children's family has now been expanded to include the fusions parent's family. Often, for emotional reasons, adults choose to split the children's families in two-the family of their mother's side and the family on their father's side.

This division may happen when the parents define the children's family as two separate entities and/or when they celebrate holidays separately. I think, as a parent, you have to stay with the idea that the children still have only one family, and this family has just expanded with new members. Although both parents may be unable to be in the same room, both parties should continuously define the family as one entity.

Both parents should be aware and accept that the children now have a larger family. I believe this is an extra benefit that will indirectly help the children to accept their new blended family members as their own, equal to the family they already have. I also think it is better for the children if the adults around them take this stance, instead of telling them "No, you can only consider A and B as your family when you are with dad, therefore we can not invite them when you are here with mom." This is not a good attitude to have, regardless of whether or not it is possible in practice for the parents to invite all of children's family to special events.

If the children insist that the whole family, including the new fusion family members, gather for an event, the parent must then be honest with the children if for some reason it is impossible to implement. If the kids are older, you must be careful with reasons such as: lack of space, money, or energy. If the reason is not true, the children will probably be very creative and come up with possible solutions in an attempt to solve the issue. Before you know it, you'll find yourself in tough predicament, which could leave the kids to believe that you don't want to celebrate the event. Therefore, it is better that the parent gives the children a brief but true version of why it is not feasible to gather everyone.

It is important to recognize your own limitations: we as parents cannot do everything for sake of the children. Some parents are able to implement such arrangements, even if they do not feel good about it, while others are unable to hide their displeasure. You should, as parents and fusion parents, recognize and respect such feelings and keep working constructively to find out how they can be minimized. In this way you can jointly plan key events for the children. I think this is the best way for the children.

Reflection

What ultimately determines if gathering everyone in the children's family is best for the well being of the children? Children can see and feel if you or the other parents do not feel good or are not happy with the joint event. Thus, the children will not enjoy it either. If that is the case, consider having two separate celebrations/events. At the same time, I think it is our duty as parents to find the best way of celebrating our children's most important events with all their family members.

5.7.7 PITFALL 7: IS IT OKAY TO TREAT THE KIDS DIFFERENTLY?

It is important to know that when you live in a blended family, both the fusion parent and the parent are allowed to treat the children differently whenever appropriate. It is obviously not good to discriminate when it comes to "ordinary" things, such as some of the kids getting candy, while others don't.

I learned very quickly that Jegwan and I had to make a distinction as to how our children were individually and how they were mentally. It is still impossible to handle every situation the right way every time. If we express love towards one child, we have to then remember to express love to the other three in order for them not to feel left out. This was difficult for us and seemed too rehearsed.

We felt it was important to attend to the children on their level and then provide exactly for their individual needs without having to distinguish whether it was justifiable with regard to the other children. The desire to always be fair can actually lead to not doing the right thing for the kids in giving them what they really want.

If you think about it, kids rarely need us to parent in the same manner and at the same level every time we are with them. The need changes a lot and depends on what the children have experienced. Sometimes you need to focus only on one child.

If you as a parent, or perhaps especially as a fusion parent, can give all the children a feeling of importance and acceptance, then you are on the right track to succeed with your fusion family.

5.7.8 PITFALL 8: WHEN THE KIDS GET EVERYTHING AND I GET "NOTHING"

As I have previously described in this book, there may be times in the blended family where you feel that the kids need all the attention and there is no time for anything else. You get "nothing" and your partner seems to have entirely forgotten about your existence.

In these situations it is important to look at the facts described in the following sections:

5.1   Rules for the blended life together
5.7   How to avoid the 10 worst pitfalls of the fusion family:
5.7.2   Pitfall 2: The kids' roles in the blended family, but what about me?

Maybe you'll find that you and your partner's previous agreements regarding spending time together after work and "adult time" have completely vanished.

Since it is difficult for both parties to guess about each other's emotional needs, as they probably aren't identical, it is important to communicate properly. Both parties must be honest about their feelings and needs for one another.

5.7.9 PITFALL 9: IF YOU HAVE A LACK OF FEELINGS FOR THE FUSION KIDS

No one can be forced to love another human being, especially when you did not choose to have that person in your life. The children did not choose their fusion parent either; the parent made that choice for them. Neither did the fusion parent choose the fusion children. At the beginning of these relationships, it is important not to expect miracles with regard to the reciprocation of feelings between fusion parents and fusion kids. Even though you love your partner, the love does not automatically extend to include love for your partner's children.

It takes time to get the relationship to evolve from the first stage, "We will behave courteously toward each other and tolerate each other," to "Now we love each other." Some fusion parents unfortunately never become fond of and/or love their fusion children. This may be acceptable to some, as long as fusion parent consistently shows a willingness to take responsibility and care for children, even though there isn't love between the parties. If you as a fusion parent feel a growing anger/irritation towards your fusion children, try to look inward in order to discover the real reason for your anger.

Ask yourself the following questions:

- Do the children respect your partner? Does your partner demand that the kids behave nicely towards you? Does your partner back you up?
- Are you jealous? Do the kids take up too much time/ space? Do you feel neglected?
- Are you angry because you are not doing all that you can?
- Do you live up to your own requirements when issues arise?

- Is there something in the upbringing of the children that may be the cause of their annoying behaviour? Is something that can be changed?
- Do the children want to achieve something specific with their behaviour?
- Are the kids jealous of you?

It is not fair to just give up right from the start because you think that the children are intolerable and you can't stand them. Part of the responsibility we implicitly assume as a fusion parent is the responsibility of working wholeheartedly to make the relationship a win-win for all parties. Therefore, as a fusion parents we must actively decide to be conflict solvers and take into account the feelings the children have in a given situation. As fusion parents, we must always try to appear positive toward our fusion children.

If it is difficult for you to get along with your fusion child, it might be a good idea to have some alone time together, just you and the child. If your fusion child is a little reluctant about this, the parent should back you up and insist that you both try. Thus, the idea will have parent's support as well. Being alone with the child can change the situation in a positive way when talking about topics that are interesting to the child.

Sulky children will find it difficult sustain being sulky if the adult is happy and unaffected by their attitude, insisting on creating a trusting and loving atmosphere. When you feel that you have a good connection with the child, you can explain to the child why you wanted to have alone time together and that you really want the two of you to get along.

At this point, if applicable, you should admit and apologize to the child if you have been unfairly mad and irritated with them. Ask the child what they honestly think about you, and tell them that you will not get mad or sad no matter what the answer. Depending on the answers received, such as: "You only punish me, not your own children, even if they do the same wrong things," or "You're really hard on me and have so many rules," or "I am afraid of you when you yell at me," you must try to be understanding and try to obtain additional clarification of the child's opinion of you.

Even though deep down you may feel you're being treated unfairly, it is important that you don't express those feelings toward the child. Instead, tell the child that you have understand them and you are sorry they feel that way, and that you promise to pay attention in the future and make an effort to correct the issues. Explain that it is your responsibility to correct a negative situation and you will not be angry if they make you aware of your perceived mistakes so you can either correct them or explain yourself.

One benefit you may encounter by spending time alone with your fusion child is the opportunity to really experience the child's personality outside the already established role in the blended family. You will find out whether or not it was the child's role or the child's perception of their role in the family that has strained your relationship.

If your impression of the child during your alone time is positive, you may find it easier to identify and understand both of your problems with the relationship. By addressing things that can move your relationship in a positive direction, you can help the child to better address their role in family and their relationship with you.

5.7.10 PITFALL 10: YOUR PARTNER'S EX SAYS: "IT'S NONE OF YOUR BUSINESS!"

As described earlier in the book, it is important that the parent and the fusion parent appear as a unit and back each other up, both in front of the children and towards the ex.

If the ex does not want the fusion parent interfering in matters with regard to their child, the parent must explain to the ex that the fusion parent has the right to do so. The parent must inform the ex about the agreement they have with the fusion parent – that the fusion parent has assumed full responsibility for the children equal to the parent him/herself. The ex therefore has to realize that the fusion parent, in some circumstances, will and should interfere when it comes to the upbringing of the children.

If the ex complains about things happening in the fusion family, the parent should explain to the ex that they fully support the fusion parent. Since your blended family must function well, it is important that you, as a parent, never talk behind the back of the fusion parent with the ex and say/admit things such as: "I don't understand why they do or say that, but I'll try to find out why."

When the parent agrees with the ex about their complaints, it can create a discord between the fusion parent and the ex, since the parent shows that they do not trust the fusion parent. This then entitles the ex to further complain about the fusion parent. The parent's loyalty should be to the fusion parent.

If the parent cannot vouch for what the fusion parent has said or done, then they should discuss this amongst themselves; never with the ex. If the fusion parent subsequently acknowledges that they have made a mistake, the parent should then apologize to the ex on behalf of both themselves and the fusion parent. The parent should always stand up for and endorse the fusion parent's words and actions.

5.8   INTERVIEW WITH A FUSION FAMILY

Dianne and Michael have been dating for two and a half years. They split up at one time, but are now moving in together. Dianne has two kids: Martin, 14 years old and Emily, 11 years old. They live with Dianne and see their dad every other weekend. Michael also has two kids: Mark, 10 and Mia, 12. Michael has the kids every other weekend at his vacation home, which is fifty miles away from where Dianne and Michael live.

Q: Have you encountered challenges with regard to the children's roles in your blended family?

Michael: *There was a period when Emily felt that I took her mother away from her.*

If we were hugging, Emily would run up and talk with Dianne. I didn't push her aside; I just stepped aside. I didn't try to stop Emily either. She is very fond of her mom.

Dianne: *In the beginning when we first time we lived together, Emily would not even talk to Michael. She said "Yes/no" and nothing else. I was deeply divided and frustrated, and spent a lot of energy on that. I believe that Emily was one of the reasons why Michael and I split up. Michael had had enough. I was torn because of her unreasonable behavior, and I did not know how to tackle it. I kept telling Emily that I loved her as much as before, even with Michael there, and that my attention towards her would not change. However, I also told her that I had the right to have an adult life. Eventually, I ended up going to a psychologist. One time I also brought Emily with me. The psychologist asked questions similar in tone, like "Do you think mom is mean? Is her boyfriend mean?" Emily was very precise with her answers. She said that Michael was nice enough but he did not need to be there, and that she had more right to me than Michael. Emily thought she could decide whom I should be with. If someone came to visit and she did not like it, she interrupted me constantly when I was talking. The psychologist explained to her that she could not make decisions for her mother. I'd been alone with Emily for eight years before I met Michael.*

Michael: *Emily had been deciding everything in her own little world. Dianne then needed to change and redefine it for her. When we split up, Dianne had a lot of fights with Emily. Emily was clinging to her and demanding a lot of attention. That was too much for Dianne. She put Emily in her place and explained to her who was in charge. After that I began to slowly come into the picture again. Since then it has gotten better. Dianne had been alone for eight years and had lived through the kids, giving them everything they wanted. She always did for herself later. So yes, the roles had to be redefined.*

Dianne: *I could do what I wanted to do when I didn't have kids.*

Michael: *I just remind Dianne that she should not forget herself in the process.*

Dianne: *You sometimes just do things without knowing why. You just do it. I wanted my life with a full-time job, two children, and homework to work out. Then you find yourself catering too much to the kids, because it's easier to do things yourself. Now I can see that it was a mistake, which I now pay for. I have also had my battles with Martin and I had to say stop. Michael made me realize this.*

Q: How do you respond in situations where your children get on each other's nerves?

Dianne: *We experienced that on vacation. I could tell that I was a little irritated at Martin and Mia when they pestered one another. But since we are not together a lot, it's okay with me.*

Michael: *I think I am a little more generous towards the kids. Let them be children. Let them be noisy and throw things around, if that is what they want.*

Dianne: *After we split up, I was better at saying "so what." I'm more relaxed now; perhaps one could say I'm relaxed in my attitude towards life and am now able to let things go. In the summer, we were together for 1-½ weeks and I could see that Emily and Martin had enough. If we had been together for a longer time, I would have ended their conflict and split them up. Done something. Done something, for example, with the girls only. I think if we had stayed together all the time, or had been under the same roof for a long time, I would probably have tried to solve the conflict. But I think it is a shame to spend time disciplining the children when they expect to have a good time. I try to help my daughter accept that she is different from Martin. She is very picky. I'm trying to get her to let go and not spend so much energy on it. Then Michael can have a little talk with Martin.*

Michael: *Martin must also stop teasing her.*

Dianne: *When we are only together on weekends, I do not think having a conflict is worth our time. What do I get out of spending a lot of energy on that? If there was a conflict with Emily and Martin, I'd just take my own daughter, calmly removing her from the situation and say, "Now you sit there."*

Q: What is your position on the financial aspects that concern the kids, i.e., whether you pay child support or not?

Dianne: *My ex pays a lot of money in child support. He even buys the clothes they need when they are with him. He likes to buy clothes for them. He also pays for Emily's horseback riding lessons. He is absolutely not cheap. I can call him and ask if he will buy winter boots for one of the children and he gladly does that. We have never discussed financial issues.*

Michael: *I pay child support to my ex. But if we are out shopping, and they want a pair of shoes, then yes, I buy them for them. If I can afford it, then I buy shoes for them. I think it's a little unfair, I cannot afford a car and I have only the vacation house, which I own. My ex is very well off now, has two cars and a big house, so I feel it is unfair that I must pay so much to her. Basically, I paid for one of their cars.*

My evaluation
Dianne's daughter Emily felt that Michael took her mother away from her and reacted very aggressively towards him.

Emily's reaction is very common in fusion families and many will recognize it. Emily felt that she 'owned' her mother because she and her brother have had her to themselves for eight years. The above is a good example of that it takes love, time and a lot of patience to redefine the children's roles from living alone to a life with a fusion parent. It is important to explain to the children what they can expect. Explain to them how their new 'worldview' seems in comparison to what they were accustomed to.

Both the adults can help the children organize their new roles in the fusion family by consistently and lovingly setting limits and requirements for their behavior.

Could Dianne and Michael have handled it differently?

If they had come to me for coaching, I would have advised them to act like a team in regards to Emily. And lovingly but firmly reject Emily when she tries to decide for them whether they can kiss and hug or not; but sometimes let her join a group-hug.

They should also not allow Emily to refuse to talk to Michael. She must understand that it is not a viable option. Conclusively, she should of course get lots of love, comfort and assurance of her mother's love, the way Dianne always has given her.

If Michael had the courage, I would advise him to directly confront Emily by insisting on talking to her without Dianne's presence. Let Emily react and maybe express all her anger at him and his intrusion into their lives. Then Michael could lovingly but firmly explain to her that he makes her mother happy and does not intent to take her mother away from her. That he is here to stay and want to contribute positively to her life. Whether he should be their lives or not, is not up to her to decide. It is the adults' decision.

Michael is bitter about having to pay so much in child support while his ex-wife lives in a financial worry-free world.

Since Michael is a little bitter about his ex's extravagant lifestyle, compared to his own, it might be worth talking to her about the possibility of reducing his child support payments, which also shows goodwill towards Dianne.

If he chooses to talk to his ex, it is a good idea NOT to focus on her lifestyle, but rather on the relationship with the children, e.g. Michael himself would like to be able to buy something for the kids. If this fails, he must accept that he can not change it and thus should not spent any more negative energy on being bitter at her.

Accept what you cannot change, give it no more of your attention and energy. You'll find out how big a relief it is to no longer use energy on being angry and bitter about something that is completely outside your control. Sometimes you can not do anything at all. Letting go creates space for new and supportive thoughts within your control.

5.9   TOOLS OF THE FUSION COACH

5.9.1   PERSONALITY TYPES AND HOW CAN THAT BE IMPORTANT TO THEM?

Living in a fusion family you might sometimes wonder which planet your partner is from since he/she can react in a certain way.

I will help you with the answer by reminding you of the fact that you two could have very different personality types.

Although you shouldn't compartmentalize one another, knowing each other's personality type is valuable information. There are many different tests available on the Internet or you can use the one described in this book.

We are all a little of everything, but there will almost always be one type you are more inclined to identify with. One of personality types will be slightly more prominent and descriptive of your personality than the others. Remember that there is no right or wrong type.

Look at the list below to find out what type you and your partner are.

DISC-Dominance, Initiative, Stability, Competence

	Dominance	Initiative	Stability	Competence
Known for	Very self-confident Selfish Resolute Goal-oriented	Self-confident Flexible Spontaneous Optimist	Stable Judicious Thoughtful Patient	Perfectionist Tactful Careful Analytical
Word & content	Bottom line Facts & theory "Non-feeling words" "Action words"	Overview Make decisions "small talk" "feeling words" Asks many questions	Fact is.... My experience is… Indirect talk Doesn't exaggerate Answers questions	We used to... Why change... Suspicious Needs documented proof
Verbal communication	Loud and direct Non-emotional Speaks clearly Direct language	Fast talker Enthusiastic Emotional Colorful language	Speaks calmly Non-emotional Soft voice	Slow talker Clear pronunciation Formal language
Body language	Self-confident Intense eye-contact Physical distance	Enthusiastic Smiles Fluttering movements	Slow movements No gestures Good eye-contact	Formal Stiff Shut off
Strong sides	Initiative Problem solver Visionary Result-oriented	Persuasive Decision maker Humorist Open & honest	Good listener Dedicated to the family Good cooperator Calm	Diplomatic High standards Follows procedures Detail-oriented

	Dominance	Initiative	Stability	Competence
Weak sides	Not a good listener Defiant Impatient Arrogant Not detail-oriented Restless	Impulsive Messy Non goal-oriented Talks a lot Too optimistic Too trusting	Resists changes Non-delegating Withholds feelings Expects orders Non deadline-oriented Focused on the past	Too critical Withholds feelings Indecisive Defensive Not responsible Authoritative
Primary needs	Control & leadership	Recognition and acceptance	Stability	Precision and quality
Primary fears	To lose control Taken advantage of	Social rejection Lose prestige	Changes Personal conflicts	Mistakes & chaos Person critique
Wants	Power & authority Status symbols New challenges Result-oriented No limitations	Popularity Freedom Cooperation Development Flexibility	Separation of job & private life Security Time to change Specific tasks Stability	Control over details Control things Overview Specializing Limited risks

Tabel 2: What type are you and your partner

When you know where you are "placed" behavior-wise in relation to each other, attitudes and opinions are easier to understand, and difficult situations will be easier to tackle. You can then ask each other the following questions:

1. Where might we encounter conflicts? Where should we be particularly cautious? Show understanding and tolerance?

2. In what areas we can complement each other with our different strengths?
3. What does it take to have our essential needs met?

When you and your partner complete this personality test it will be stored in your memory as a tool, ready to be applied in helping to understand why you are different. It is also worth remembering that differences strengthen your relationships if they are recognized and accepted.

5.9.2 THE WAY TO GOOD COMMUNICATION

There will be many sensitive topics to discuss in the fusion family. With this comes the risk that productive communication might dissolve.

In situations where you feel accused or when your children have come under your partner's microscope, you might find yourself in a huge drama defending yourself and your children. You'll start digging a deep defensive trench, as will your partner. The trench war has begun, and it can be very hurtful and hard to escape.

What goes wrong every time?

My own story
I consistently commit two major mistakes. I bring past and similar situations into the discussion, rather than being neutral with regard to what is happening in the present. I feel that I need to put more weight behind my words in order to be understood, and I need to point out where things went wrong in the past.

I often find myself justifying my role in the conflict, leading me to feel incredibly sorry for myself. I play the role of a victim and cast Jegwan as the villain. Does this pattern seem familiar to you? If we become aware of our own patterns and the roles we play, we are already attempting to break the patterns that create unhealthy and devastating communication in the fusion family.

Below I've listed a few roles. Try to figure out what roles you and your partner play when you are having arguments.

The following four roles are barriers for good communication in the fusion family:

1. 5.9.3   Assuming the role of the victim
2. 5.9.4   Using guilt against others
3. 5.9.5   Using force
4. 5.9.6   Wanting to be right all the time

5.9.3   ASSUMING THE ROLE OF THE VICTIM

Characteristics:
- Complaining
- Feeling sorry for yourself
- Feeling hurt
- Feeling frustrated
- Crying
- Getting angry

There are reasons why you have you have assumed this role. Maybe you believe things should be different, or that things are hurtful to you or that your partner is trying to hurt you.

Ask yourself: "Is this who I am... a helpless victim who feels sorry for myself?" Then, try to think, "It is what it is... I have a choice."

5.9.4   USING GUILT AGAINST OTHERS

Characteristics:
- Pestering
- Distorting things
- Trying to hurt someone
- Feeling sorry for yourself and whining

If you use guilt against others, you are not honest. You may try to get your partner to feel uncomfortable in the hope that they will be pressured to do or feel something in particular. Is it really your intent to make your partner feel uncomfortable? You may ask yourself: "Is this who I am? Am I really a dishonest person without integrity? Would I allow someone to be dishonest with me?" Instead of using guilt, tell your partner honestly and directly how you really feel.

5.9.5 USING FORCE

Characteristics:
- When offended, you get angry or shout
- Attacking and/or hurting your partner
- Forcing your partner to adapt
- Oppressing your partner

If you use force against your partner, it's almost always impossible to achieve your goals in discussing issues. It always has the opposite effect. If you scream at your partner, they will get defensive and stop listening, and instead focus on stopping your anger. Anger won't get you any closer to your original objective of the discussion.

Before you start speaking about a sensitive topic with your partner, remind yourself of your old patterns and make a conscious decision not to fall into the same communication traps as you had in the past.

5.9.6 WANTING TO BE RIGHT ALL THE TIME

Characteristics:
- Always thinking you know best about how things should be done
- Always having to have the last word in a discussion
- Keeping a record of everything
- Withholding emotionally
- Being judgmental

One issue that you will often discuss in a fusion family merger is the distribution of the practical tasks – who does what, and how tasks are performed. You must be willing to delegate and let go of your need to control things to be done exactly your way. You will not able to love your partner completely until you stop judging them and instead accept them as they are.

"What is the purpose of being in control? What do I get out of it?" Try to practice letting go of your control over your world. You may be surprised that you feel relieved. Try to, just for a day or two, accept your partner as they are. When we are aware of the roles we play, we have the ability to change them.

Reflection

We can choose NOT to assume the same role the next time we are having a discussion with our partner. It might sound and feel strange knowing that we have a choice because we often feel that we don't. We feel we are being drawn into the discussion without wanting to. For the most part, we believe that deep feelings come before our thoughts. I believe it is vice versa-it's the thought that creates the feeling.

When we keep reacting to our partner, we give them the power to determine our internal state of mind. This does not create the best basis for healthy communication within our relationship. With that in mind, we can now decide that from now on, we will make a choice. It will most likely not happen as often as desired, but when you do succeed, remember to notice the feeling of freedom it gives you in being aware and in control of your inner state of mind. Instead of simply reacting to what happens, be conscious about it and act accordingly.

6. HOW TO CREATE A GOOD FOUNDATION

6.1 THE 8 GREATEST GIFTS FOR THE FUSION FAMILY

As difficult as it is to be in a blended family, you can do a lot of things to create a sense of belonging. One way is choosing to invest time alone with your fusion children. This section gives you ideas for the "gifts" you can give to your fusion family. Find out what works for your family.

6.1.1 GIFT 1: CREATING TRADITIONS IN THE BLENDED FAMILY

Creating entirely new traditions for your blended family is nice for both children and adults. It gives everyone a sense of belonging when they can look forward to something the family has planned together.

Below are examples of new traditions you can introduce that will be a great framework for the future:

- On children's birthdays, put a wreath of flowers around the birthday child's plate and have them sit on a specially decorated "Royal" chair. Put a flag on your car when you drive with the birthday child.

- Assign one day per year that is named after each child, for example, "Jonas Day." On this day, the child spends time exclusively with the parent and the fusion parent, and the parents only do things in the interest of that child.

- Have a sleepover where all the children may have one or two friends over.

- Have a specific theme for the weekend, for example: a gaming weekend where there are tables set up and games take place in various locations in the house.

- Have a picnic on a blanket in the living room instead of eating at the dining table.

- Put the children's names into a hat and then draw a random name. The lucky child gets breakfast in bed on Sunday.

- Introduce multi-colored afternoon drinks for the whole family on Friday afternoon.

- Establish a day for the whole family to play games together.

There are unlimited possibilities in creating new traditions for your fusion family, and kids will love and welcome them. When you hear the kids happily talk about the traditions with their friends, you'll know you've attained your goals.

6.1.2   GIFT 2: MAKING ORDINARY THINGS IMPORTANT

My own story

"Making ordinary things special" was an expression I only fully understood the importance of when I moved in with Jegwan about six years ago.

He inherited from his loving mother the unique ability to talk so interestingly about a box of cars that even I (almost) wanted to play with it. With great enthusiasm, Jegwan told my boys about the amazing metal box he owned which held tanks, soldiers, and other military toys from his childhood. The more his story progressed, the more wide my boys' eyes became. I was able to predict what would happen when Jegwan's story was over, and sure enough they eagerly asked if they could borrow the metal box, promising they would take really good care of everything. They just had to play with something so amazing. The metal box of cars will always be something special – and because they were allowed to play with that box, they were special as well.

I was very inspired by his story and I decided immediately to follow his example, so I hurried over to my parents' house and found my old beloved Smurfs, which I also put in an interesting box. I was not as good at selling my Smurfs to the kids, since I could not remember anything other than the name of the "old Smurf." The children were not as enthusiastic as I hoped they'd be.

> **Reflection**
> Enthusiasm and empathy can create really great moments for the fusion family. Try looking around in drawers and cupboards for an item you can make special for your family. You will smile at the result and ask why you didn't do this a long time ago.

6.1.3 GIFT 3: A FUSION PARENT CAN FIND HIS/HER OWN NICHE

If you as a fusion parent have an interest in something that you love to do because it makes you happy and comfortable, introduce it to your fusion children. It may be that you have a special hobby or are particularly passionate about cooking or home decoration. The action isn't crucial in itself; what matters is the kids can sense your enthusiasm. Show them your enthusiasm and have them participate. Try to create something that you share with your fusion children, something that is yours and theirs only.

If you cannot think of any topics you can introduce to your fusion children, here are some helpful questions to ask yourself:

- When you as a child and/or teenager forgot about time and place and was completely engulfed, what did you do?
- Did you have a collection of some sort?
- What were you doing in your spare time?
- Which hobbies did you have?
- What do you know a lot about?
- If you had an extra hour without interruption to talk about anything you want, what would that be?
- Which magazines do you like to read? Why?
- If you were to go to a lecture, what would it be about?
- Which famous person would you really like to meet? And why?
- Which movies do you like to watch? Why?
- What do you do when you're home alone?

I hope my questions have fueled your creativity and given you some ideas on how to create some private space just for you and your fusion kids. Perhaps you will reconnect with a passion you once had and which you completely have forgotten about.

6.1.4 GIFT 4: DOING SOMETHING SPECIAL WITH THE FUSION CHILD

A great way to get to know your fusion child is to do something special with only that child.

For example tell the child that the two of you are going to a concert by the child's favorite band or that you're seeing a show at the theater. Doing this sends a very important message, causing the child to think: "You have taken time out from the rest of the family because you want to do something special with me. When you do that, you show me that you love me and that makes me happy."

It is important to find activities which are of special interest to the fusion child. This helps you both to feel comfortable. When you take the child to the activity, you should tell the other kids that you will also take them to an activity that you know will interest them. Explain to them that they will have to take turns depending on the activity, and that the adults will let them know when it is their turn. The children might be a little upset in the beginning and think it isn't fair, but when the day comes that it is their turn, they will be happy to come home and share their experiences with the other children.

6.1.5   GIFT 5: LETTING GO OF HABITS AND LETTING THE FUSION PARENT INSPIRE YOU

While you may experience very difficult times in your fusion family, times that feel hopeless and confusing, there will also be many new positive experiences for the whole family to discover.

It is a privilege for the fusion parent to be allowed to contribute to and influence the fusion kids' lives with new ideas and initiatives that differ from those to which they are accustomed. But when you have set habits, you might not always be willing to change the way you do things. You are comfortable with your ways, and therefore are not willing to change. It is not difficult to imagine the outcome if both parents insist on their way of doing things.

My own story
I was a slave to habits and always did things in the same order, at the same time, every single day. I was very structured and planned my life in detail both for the kids and me. These rituals resulted in that I often would stress out both the children and myself with my many "need-to-dos" that needed to be done in order for me to feel that things were okay. When things were finally done, we also had to enjoy ourselves because now we deserved it. Unfortunately, we often ran out of time.

Jegwan was just the opposite. He rarely did things in the same order, and certainly not at the same time if he didn't feel like it. I remember a situation where I became really frustrated with his ability to completely forget about time and instead be present in the moment. Jegwan and Nicklas were having a really good conversation about a topic that interested Nicklas. At first I enjoyed looking at them and listening in, but slowly the evening's chores came to my mind: Clear the table, wash the dishes, make lunches, and bath for Nicklas – all this had to be completed by 8p.m.!

All of these thoughts got the best of me and I started acting on them. Jegwan looked up at me with a wrinkle in his forehead and explained to me that they were talking about something important and suggested that if Nicklas skipped the bath it wouldn't hurt him. I was shocked and explained to Jegwan that Nicklas couldn't just skip the bath. He just looked at me with incomprehension, and asked why not. He added with a smile that Nicklas seemed fine and clean to him. I was still not entirely convinced but said okay, though I felt bad because things were not the way they were "supposed to be."

That evening we discussed that I thought Jegwan was too strong with his attitude about practical things. He thought that I always was stressing about how practical things had to be done in a certain order and at a certain time. We agreed that there was a place for both his and my attitude in our everyday lives and that we had to find a compromise we both could live with.

For my part, it meant that I had to be a little more lenient in my requirements for what and when things had to be done if it was at the expense of something far more important to the family's well being. We agreed that it was important for our family to have the opportunity to immerse ourselves in something important or interesting.

Think of this question: Where in your life would you really benefit from loosen up or letting go of something. Where could you really release some negative energy and turn it into something more fruitful. I am sure there are issues you just have adopted from your parents without even questioning, if it also works for you and if it fits your own family values. What is really the worst thing that can happen, if you let go of some of your bad habits and patterns? What is your honest answer to this question?

> **Reflection**
> Habits and patterns are difficult to change and it often takes time before you really feel comfortable with the change. Let the fusion parent inspire you to do things in a new way – it's good for both children and adults. You may feel relieved getting rid of some old habits and patterns.

6.1.6 GIFT 6: THE FUSION PARENT CAN ADD A LITTLE SPICE TO THE KIDS' LIFE

In your role as a parent, you are probably your own worst enemy when it comes to assessing whether you have succeeded in that role or not. You may feel inadequate if you don't always manage to stimulate and encourage children all the time. Therefore, the fusion parent can often contribute new dimensions to the lives of the parent and the kids.

The fusion parent will often have both a different view of many situations and an entirely different way of handling them. The fusion parent has the opportunity to add a little spice to the children's lives on emotional, practical, and entertainment levels. On the emotional level, the fusion parent can contribute with stories of their life experiences that most likely are very different from the parent's.

The fusion parent may have some experiences that can help children in certain situations that are completely different from the parent's. The deep emotional bond you have with your children can stand in the way of all rational thinking when trying to handle a situation concerning them. Therefore, the fusion parent will sometimes be much better at handling issues where you as a parent might feel: "I am the parent and although I may not be thinking rationally I must save my children from outside world." On a practical level, the fusion parent can give new insight and ideas to the many routines and chores of daily life.

My own story

If your children are young, here's a cute idea you might find useful:

I remember one evening when Jegwan was making lunches for the next day, I came into the kitchen to see how he was doing. He was about to draw on the hard-boiled eggs and I asked him, of course, why he was doing that. He explained to me that it was for Jonas and that the egg had an angry man on one side and a happy man on the other side.

I thought it was a very cute idea and told Jonas of the egg when I put him to bed that evening. The next day when I drove Jonas to kindergarten, I had forgotten all about the funny egg in the lunchbox, but Jonas had not. When we arrived at school, he ran into the room and summoned all his young companions, whereupon he put his lunchbox on a chair. His friends stood in a circle around the chair, and when Jonas asked if they were ready they said yes. He ripped the lid off of the lunchbox and took out the funny egg, showing them the happy man on one side and the angry man on the other. His friends eagerly commented: Ah, that is so cool, I wish it were mine, I want to bring one like that tomorrow!

I had never thought of making a sweet egg like that, but Jegwan, Jonas' fusion dad, did.

> **Reflection**
> When it comes to entertainment the fusion parent can make a difference for the kids. They have the opportunity to put their own fingerprints on many areas and situations for the fusion children where the parent may not have sufficient insight or empathy to be actively supportive of the children's many interests.

The fusion parent can complement the parent by making the children's lives more diverse. Similarly, the fusion parent can show the kids values and traditions from their own childhood and maybe teach them some things they are good at from which the children can benefit.

The fusion parent can tell their own childhood stories from when they were the same age as the children. A fusion parent can be a great inspiration to the children. One day you might be surprised by all the new projects the children have started – How did they get that idea? It's awesome and they look like they are having fun.

6.1.7 GIFT 7: THE EX THINKS THAT THE FUSION PARENT IS THE ONLY ONE WHO CAN SOLVE PROBLEMS

Another problem that might occur in the fusion family is that your ex believes that the fusion parent is the only one who can solve problems and handle situations that arise with the children. The ex no longer trusts or has confidence in you as a parent, and therefore refuses any communication with you and will only speak with the fusion parent since they are the most rational adult.

If the fusion parent wants to, they may well choose to deal with the ex, although it may seem a little awkward to discuss your partner's children with their ex. But some communication between the ex and the fusion parent is preferable compared to no communication at all. This solution actually happens and can be beneficial, because there are no hurt feelings involved that could affect and ruin the cooperation with regard to the children. The fusion parent can objectively clarify and assess the different situations without looking for any "hidden" agendas, which the parent might have done. If the parent in the fusion family previously spent a lot of energy trying to figure out their ex's agendas, this solution may also end up creating more peace and harmony for the fusion family. The parent will be relieved of the heavy task of communicating with the ex who no longer listens to them anyway. If the ex no longer wants to be in contact with the parent, it is worth considering whether the fusion parent should be in charge of the communication with the ex.

6.1.8 GIFT 8: APPRECIATING EACH OTHER IN YOUR NEW ROLES AS FUSION PARENTS

It is worth remembering that the moment you become a blended family, the most important thing is no longer the fusions parent's love for the parent. Now, the fusion parent's relationship with the children is more crucial, and determines whether the love between the adults will last. With this in mind it is very important, especially in the beginning, to appreciate each other in your new roles as fusion parents.

Your role a mother or father is a given and you might not always be praised for filling this role. But in the role of a fusion parent, you will not only both expect and need recognition and feedback from one another, but also from the outside world. The fusion parent may often feel insecure, especially if they do not have kids. So to overcome this insecurity, it is a good idea to praise each other in front of the children.

If you as a fusion parent have handled a situation well, the parent should notice and show their delight with regard to your effort. The more the parent recognizes and observes the fusion parent's effort, the more safe and secure the fusion parent will feel in their new role. The motivation to establish a close relationship with the children increases significantly when you feel appreciated and recognized.

My own story

Even after several years as a fusion mom to Oscar and Andrea, I still need Jegwan's recognition of my role. I do not fulfil my role as a fusion mom with the same ease I fulfill my role of being a mother to my children, Nicklas and Jonas. Therefore, I ask Jegwan lots of questions to find out whether he agrees with me. However, I have often had to admit that I have a tendency to over-interpret his answer when it comes to situations about Oscar and Andrea. Doubt will often bother me – whether I have said or done the right thing. If it was about Nicklas or Jonas, I never had a shadow of doubt.

I expected that after many years in this role as a fusion mom, I would have achieved the same confidence I have in my role as mother of Nicklas and Jonas. But I have to admit that I still need to be recognized as a fusion mom.

> **Reflection**
> I recommend that you show appreciation of each other in your roles as fusion parents so the uncertainty often associated with your roles is eliminated. Sparring, praising and recognition are very important for the fusion family in order to become a fully integrated family.

6.2 INTERVIEW WITH A FUSION DAD

Thomas lives with Anne and Anne's daughter Eline, who is three and a half years old. They have lived together for a half year.

Question to Thomas: How have you defined your role as a fusion dad compared to Eline's biological father?

Thomas: *I've been very careful to let Eline know that I am aware of who her biological father is. I consider myself Eline's friend Thomas. I do not represent anything more than her biological father does.*

I have spent a lot of time with Eline and I haven't thought about how I should be different from her father. It's been a natural process.

We've played a lot together, games that I thought were fun when I was a child. Maybe there will be a need for more conversations about this topic when Eline is older and wonders why she does not live with her biological father.

Q: Have you added anything new to Eline's life?

Thomas: *I think I'm pretty good at playing with Eline. We play various things. I've had a different upbringing and the things I do are often a little sillier. There are also games I played when I was a kid, which I play now with Eline, because I think there are funny. Anne does not play those games with her.*

Anne adds: *Thomas is better at playing with Eline than I am. He is much more into the game, giving them a very close connection. Thomas has more patience while playing and feels like playing for much longer than I do.*

Thomas: *I also think it is a really good idea to do things with Eline without Anne. It strengthens our relationship, and when her mother is not nearby she has to listen to what I say. This is somewhat easier because she can't just turn to mom all the time.*

We have developed a game where Eline is the adult and goes to work and I am the child who gets picked up from kindergarten. When I get picked up from kindergarten, I tell her what I did that day. And then the game starts all over again. Eline loves this game, and we spend a lot of time playing it.

Anne comments: *Eline thinks that Thomas is better at certain things, including driving a car, swinging on swings, etc.*

Q: If you were to give a new fusion parent good advice, what would it be?

Thomas: *If you both agree to being on equal terms, participating in activities, getting together for social events-all this has to be in place in order to become more integrated as a family.*

I do not think you should insist on being called mom or dad, but rather show that you know you are not the child's biological parent. I also think it is important to do things alone with your fusion child; do new and different things. This is a good idea because it will bring you closer. I also think you should accept that you are not a world champion in the first month of being a fusion parent.

Question to Anne: What has been your biggest concern with regard to Eline having a fusion dad?

Answer: *My biggest concern has been whether Thomas liked Eline. Also, if we were to have our own children, I have been worried if Thomas would like them more than Eline. It is actually okay if Thomas loves Eline less than his biological children, because I do not think he would give her less love anyway. There is much love between Eline and Thomas otherwise I would feel bad in certain situations.*

Thomas comments: *I had thought you would have replied to that question by saying that you wanted to make sure I do not get tired of her, while you at the same time must attend to Eline's needs. You are always in a dilemma.*

Q: What are your requirements/expectations for Thomas in his role as a fusion dad?

Anne: *From the beginning I had very clear requirements for a man I would be with, for example, he had to be willing to engage in the parental role and take part in my child's life. I would not compromise on those points. He would also have to like my child, otherwise I could not be with him. He should treat Eline respectfully, thoughtfully, and lovingly otherwise it was not going to work out.*

Thomas comments: *If it had not worked between Eline and I, Anne and I would probably not be together now.*

Anne says: *I had not anticipated that Thomas would take as much responsibility as he does. I had absolutely no expectations. I count* *myself lucky every day that he does take responsibility. It is quite unique and incredible.*

My evaluation
Thomas spends a lot of alone time with Eline.

Thomas' answers in the interview emphasize the importance of a fusion parent being willing to invest time and energy in the children, with and without the parent present.

If we want a good and healthy relationship with our fusion children, we need to spend time getting to know them by doing things together, even without the parent. Show them both in speech and action that we choose to involve them in our lives. Thomas has done that and the outcome is positive.

In the interview, Thomas and Anne state that Eline has already indicated, that after half a year with Thomas, there are things he does better than her mom and that he is also funnier than to her mom.

We can help the children to see the benefits of having a new adult in their lives. Helping them to see that mom/dad is a happier parent if she/he is with the fusion parent. Open their eyes to the possibility of getting something different, new and exciting in their lives.

If the children are older, they might also see the advantage of talking with the fusion parent about things they might not want to involve the parent in.

Anne's demands, expectations and main concerns about the relationship between Thomas and Eline.

Anne's concern of Thomas not liking Eline, is one she shares with most parents, who are part of a new fusion family. It's our worst fear that our partner does not see the qualities we see in our children. We almost desire to highlight and emphasize their positive traits as a teaser to "sell" our children to the partner.

As a parent we have to accept that we have these feelings and ask ourselves what it takes for those feelings diminish or disappear altogether? We need to communicate that clearly.

We might need our partner to tell us about the positive experiences he/she has had with our children. The more appreciative and accepting he/she is towards our children, the more we can relax in our "monitoring role." We should let our partner know how we feel.

Anne says in the interview, that she has accepted the idea that Thomas might not love Eline as much as the children they may have together in the future.

So many parents know these feelings. If you want to have children together, it is a good idea to think through this scenario and exert yourself to accept the fact, that you can NOT force your partner to love your own child. However, you CAN expect that he/she does not discriminate when it comes to physical care of and attention given to both his/her biological children and the fusion children.

6.3 TOOLS OF THE FUSION COACH: THE WAY TO ACHIEVE A GREAT RELATIONSHIP

When we are in a relationship, and especially in a fusion family, we find ourselves challenged in many ways and "drama" may often occur more often than usual.

One of the first things we do is evaluate our partner: are they good enough, do they come from a normal or abnormal family, are they sweet, are their children well-behaved, etc. We spend lots of time trying to stay ahead to predict how and what our partner will say and do in a given situation. We spend most of our energy evaluating every situation and action. Often this is not deliberately done, and when we react it's to things we only imagine about each other. We create positive and negative lists with things such as willingness to clean, being responsible for the children, etc.

It is worthwhile to pause for a moment and ask yourself these questions:

- How much time do I spend daily creating lists for my partner and their children?
- Is this really the way I want to be in our relationship?
- How would I feel if my partner judged me this way?

Is it really true that my partner will gain points in this system I have invented, and needs these points in order for us to have a good relationship? (My partner does not even know my system/lists!)

Our lists can also be called our "rules". If we are not aware of them, these rules may control the way we act in our relationship. We should instead be relating to reality, not the rules/lists we made up. The first step to have a really good relationship is to train ourselves to step away from these rules and into reality. An effective way to do this is to relate to the actuality of a situation without making up a "story", and then give the situation a particular value, either negative or positive.

Imagine the following:

You come home from work and find your partner asleep on the couch, the house a mess, the laundry still in the washing machine, and the kids dirty.

How do you react?

1. You react the same as you did last time: have a fit and shout at him for being irresponsible, selfish, and lazy. Why do you have to do everything around the house?

Or do you:

2. Breathe deeply and think. What is the reality here? My partner asleep, the house is messy, the kids are dirty, the fridge is empty. What do I need most of all right now? Which "outcome" do I want right now? And what do I think my partner needs right now?

Reality is what it is. "I need to take a nice hot bath with a glass of red wine." So do what you need to do. The result I want is to have a nice and cozy evening with my partner and our children.

Ask yourself: What will it take for me to achieve this?

Try to put yourself in your partner's shoes by thinking "Maybe my partner need to rest a bit. Perhaps I should let him be or maybe give him a kiss on the cheek and ask if he wants a glass red wine."

Do something different than the norm-breaking your own patterns may be what it takes to transform your relationship. The difference is to deal with reality as it is, rather than how reality should look like according to your rules. If you are able to keep drama at a distance, you will have a better and more solid foundation for your relationship.

There are plenty of sensitive topics for the fusion family, and most of us know when and how to have the best conversations to achieve the best results and solutions for our practical and emotional life – and the best time is never when we just react to something.

A good question to ask yourself is:

Would you still be with your partner if they never change?

It obviously requires mental energy and willpower to act and react differently from the way you are used to. But I believe it takes less energy compared to when you are angry and thus ruin the good mood for the evening. Therefore, I think it is a really good investment to break away from the negative way of reacting.

7. LIFE IN THE FUSION FAMILY AND POSSIBLE PROBLEMS

7.1. HOW TO REFER TO THE ADULTS AROUND THE KIDS AND HOW TO LEAVE YOUR KID/KIDS WITH THE FUSION PARENT WITHOUT FEELING GUILTY

When you want to integrate the children, it is a good idea right from the start to decide how you want the children to refer to you and your partner, and also how they refer to the children's other parents.

In a fusion family, the parent often feels that they cannot ask their partner to baby-sit their children. The parent will often worry about whether they are a burden to their partner and therefore won't be able to do anything without the children.

I think this sentence is quite common, "Is it okay if the kids stay here with you while I run an errand?" The parent feels that the children are their responsibility and do not see their partner in the same light as the children's biological parent. The parent then chooses to just bring the kids with them because they don't feel that it's okay to ask the partner to baby-sit them. The parent often takes this unnecessary precaution in order to not "burden" their partner with their children.

It would be a relief for both the parent and the partner if this issue can be resolved. It is probably only the parent who perceives this as "babysitting", whereas the partner probably just feels that they are at home with the children while the parent is out, and is therefore not a babysitting service but something quite natural. Both the parent and the fusion parent must work together to entrust their children to each other without feeling guilty. Both parents in the fusion family should be able to do something away from home without their respective children.

How to refer to the adults around the kids - my own story

I have learned that Jegwan's and my lack of awareness and choices in how we have referred to one another has influenced the children, and now is very difficult to correct. One day I began to notice the way we refer to each other in our fusion family. When you live in a nuclear family, parents often refer to each other around the children as mom or dad: "Ask mom/dad if they can do this or that."

When Nicklas and Jonas talked to Jegwan, they suddenly began to refer to me as Charlotte. Jonas would ask: "Jegwan, where is Charlotte?" Jonas would never have referred to me as Charlotte if he was asking his dad; he would have asked: "Daddy, where is mom?"

Of course, the reason for this new reference was that, to Oscar and Andrea I was "Charlotte" and not "Mom," and when Nicklas and Jonas mentioned me to them I was indeed "Charlotte" again and not "Mom". Oscar and Andrea could not tell Jonas that he should ask "mom" about this or that, but instead that he had to ask "Charlotte."

And what about Jegwan? What did he call me? He also told Nicklas and Jonas that they should ask Charlotte about something, not mom... so I then understood why I had partially lost my "status" as a mother. I had no desire to be reduced to Charlotte as I had always felt pride and joy being called mom. I spoke to Jegwan about this and he promised to try to remember not to call me Charlotte when he referred to me in front of Nicklas and Jonas. It went very well for a while, although instead of Charlotte he would say: You can ask YOUR mother. When I heard this I felt a little distanced as a mother and deprived of all the privileges that come with motherhood in a family.

> **Reflection**
> When adults refer to each other, I think it is better to remove YOUR and just say mom or dad. It will probably feel awkward at first, but I think it will ultimately provide the entire family with a wonderful sense of unison.

When it comes to the exes, the parent in the fusion family will naturally say to the children: Tomorrow you are going to mom/dad's house. The fusion parent will often say to the fusion children: Tomorrow you are going to YOUR mom/dad's house. In this situation, I think it's a good idea if both parent and fusion parent choose to refer to the other parent as mom or dad, and not use the word YOUR. This reference is natural if you see from the children's point of view.

Not all parents are concerned about these referral issues, but it may good to consider how you feel about this topic. For me, it was important to try to use the terminology used in nuclear families.

7.2   INTERVIEW WITH A FUSION FAMILY

Thomas lives with Anne and Anne's daughter Eline, who is three and a half years old. They have lived together for a half year.

Question for Anne, mother of Eline: Do you feel that Thomas is babysitting Eline when you go out? Are there other areas where you have felt the difference of your child living with a fusion parent versus her biological parent?

Answer: *It is a little different. If I see that Thomas is very tired, I take Eline with me and don't even ask whether it would be okay if she stayed at home. I do not know whether I would do the same if it were her biological father. I might. There have been situations where I took it for granted when she stayed home with him, but I am a little more observant now.*

On Saturday I will be at an event and we haven't decided whether Thomas actually should spend his Saturday evening watching MY child. I am a little concerned about whether I should go or if I should stay home this time. So even though Thomas is included on equal terms, I feel that it is not completely okay, that there is a difference. If he had been her biological father I would say, well, of course it is his responsibility as well. So yes, there is a difference.

With regard to bringing and picking up Eline I feel that it always has to be me, but I also know that I do not have to feel that way because Thomas will take responsibility. If I have an evening lecture or something else, I wonder if it's okay to ask Thomas to baby-sit or if I should hire a babysitter. But it also seems a little odd. If I were alone, I'd hire a babysitter or if I was with her biological father, I would just say that I had to go.

Thomas comments: *It you're going to party or something in the evening and it is my responsibility to watch her, I sometimes feel that it is a little hard or a little strange. However, if I had to go somewhere, I would not think about it, I must admit. Maybe it's also because I have concerns about how it will turn out with Eline and me, because at the moment Anne is the one who reads bedtime stories. What if we have a conflict and she does not want to go to bed? I do sometimes feel that I am a babysitter. However, if we do hire a babysitter, I feel that I fail as a fusion dad. I chose to be with Anne and chose to say yes to the whole package. I chose to have this particular child with Anne.*

Anne: *When Eline is on vacation with her dad for three weeks, I miss her immensely. It makes Thomas a little weary to see and hear me like this, because we instead could enjoy being alone together.*

Thomas comments: *I understand Anne and I miss Eline too, just not the same way. It might annoy me a bit when we have a weekend without her – that Anne can't wait until Eline comes home while I am sad that the weekend is already over.*

My evaluation
Anne does not expect Thomas to babysit Eline, although they are on equal terms.

One thing is the decision about having joint responsibility. Thomas and Anne did make that decision. Another thing is the emotions in regards to that decision, both Anne's and Thomas' emotions.

They both know logically that they have agreed to share responsibilites. So why is it still hard to feel that Thomas is not babysitting? It is difficult for them to accept how they both feel about this since both parties expected that the "real" emotions would be completely in place at the time they made their decision.

It takes time for decisions, actions and emotions to be in harmony.

Our feelings do not always follow at the same pace as our decision-making. It takes time before you feel the consequences of the decision of joint responsibility, because it is different for both of them. Anne was accustomed to do everything herself and Thomas only had himself to care for. It takes time to feel comfortable with the consequences of change and we cannot force or stress ourselves through it, but only live through it.

If Anne and Thomas want to live with the decision of joint responsibility in a logical way, they must talk from time to time and be honest about the expectations and feelings, they experience in a given situation.

Anne will allow Thomas to sulk over having to babysit Eline, but he has to do it anyway. Reversely Anne can tell Thomas that babysitting Eline should not be her sole responsibility. As Eline gets older and becomes less dependent on babysitting, the emotions will subside and maybe eventually completely disappear.

Anne and Thomas can also choose a different option. They can choose to accept that their feelings are different from one another; Anne accepts babysitting of Eline as her responsibility and Thomas admits that he feels he's babysitting, despite his "yes" to the joint responsibility.

A "yes" to the shared responsibility of course does not necessarily mean that it is applicable in all the circumstances surrounding the child. There may be exceptions in order to make life a little easier. You can always choose to make adjustments on the joint responsibility over time.

7.3 HOW TO REPRIMAND EACH OTHER'S KIDS AND HOW TO HAVE CONFIDENCE IN YOUR PARTNER WHEN THEY REPRIMAND YOUR KIDS

In the beginning you will often find it hard to get yourself to reprimand your fusion children, even though deep down you know that had it been your own child who had done or said the same, you would have responded immediately.

You might find yourself in a situation where you take your frustrations out on your own children because it is easier to reprimand them in hope that the reprimand will indirectly affect your fusion kids.

Trusting that your partner sees your children's well being as a priority is probably one of the most difficult things for a parent to do, as well as trusting that their intentions are genuine and loving when they choose to reprimand your children.

Immediately, one can perhaps be led to believe that moving in together is a clear signal that you both choose each other, each other's kids, and this new life. However, I myself had to realize that it takes much more than that. The feeling of complete confidence in your partner and in their relationship to your children can only be created by unconditional and sustained commitment to the children, and through loving acts and words that show that your children have the same priority as your partner's own children.

My own story

This situation is shaky and unfair, but I felt this way in the beginning about Andrea and Oscar. I could not bring myself to scold or reprimand them because they were so sweet and easy to deal with in many respects.

In the specific situation where I should have reacted, my response was not forthcoming because they had just sat and cuddled with Jonas and asked me if they could help. They had also set the table, which I had told them to do. I always had a good reason ready, and therefore thought it was okay that I did not reprimand them.

For a long time I just tried to bear with them without saying anything, until Jegwan one day demanded to know what was wrong since I was in such a bad mood. I explained the situation to him, and when he asked how I had handled it, I gave him the same reasons I used: That I could not bring myself to reprimand Oscar and Andrea as it would make me feel stingy and bad if I did.

Jegwan looked at me and said, "That's not going to work. You have to confront them. They can feel that you're in a bad mood and they have a right to know what they did wrong. You have to be straightforward and let them know the way you would towards your own boys." I knew deep down that he was right, but I had to be ready before I was able to make an active decision about exerting myself with regard to Andrea and Oscar. I eventually succeeded, but it required some hard work as it didn't come naturally to reprimand them in the same way I reprimanded my own boys.

It is one thing not to able to reprimand your fusion children – it is another thing not to be allowed. There are some fusion families who share this task among themselves: You take care of your children and their upbringing, and I take care of my children and their upbringing. I have tried to find out how to effectively implement this method without conflicts, such as when the parent is not present and thus unable to reprimand their children. As I have described, I believe that when a situation arises for the fusion parent, then they must resolve it. In addition, the parent and the fusion parent might have different limitations for what they think is okay, just as they may have different expectations for their children.

Another dilemma for the fusion family is when the children are only there every other weekend and the parent consistently refuses to reprimand and correct the children. Because they are there for such a short time, the parent doesn't want to ruin the mood by reprimanding them. This sentiment is understandable, but not sustainable in the long run. When you only have the children every other weekend, you should still maintain your roles as a fusion parent/parent and raise awareness of exactly the same things and situations as you would if you had the kids full time. This creates confidence within the children, and helps them to recognize the parent and fusions parent's limitations, instead of being permitted to "run wild" every other weekend. We do NOT do the kids any favours by being lenient and extra tolerant towards them if we would behave differently had they been with us full time. The amount of time you spend with your children should not play into how you reprimand them, even though deep down you would prefer to shrug and say: I don't see them very often and they will be leaving soon, so I don't have the heart to say anything. It would be different if I saw them more frequently.

For my part, I behaved almost like a mother hen with regard to my own children. Every time I heard a sound coming from Jegwan, I immediately defended my kids. I simply could not stand when he reprimanded my boys – I got a stomach-ache and couldn't keep quiet. In fact, every time he did it, I was mad at him for a long time. I felt better if I reprimanded them. My kids knew me and were comfortable with my temperament, but they didn't know Jegwan as well, of course, and they sometimes felt insecure and scared when he scolded them. I even told Jegwan that I was perfectly capable of reprimanding my boys, and if I said nothing to them it was because there was nothing to be said. I would then nonchalantly flip my hair and ask if we agreed on this. We did not! I was wrong! I knew this deep inside, but I still chose my way of thinking.

One day the situation was reversed. I reprimanded Oscar, after which Jegwan immediately became defensive. I could not help but smile because I knew all too well the mechanisms working inside him the moment I put a finger on one of his darlings. The result of this was that we went for a long walk and talked it through. We agreed it was hard to experience your partner reprimanding your children while you sit there listening, not being able to interfere.

Jegwan began by saying that if all six of us are to live together, it is necessary for both of us to educate and reprimand each other's children, and learn to be at peace with it. It was important for our families well being that we both be allowed to speak freely to each other's children. Jegwan and I had different boundaries and different perceptions of what was important for us in the upbringing of our respective children. Some things irritate and annoy me and not him, and vice versa. We agreed to use the following method until we both felt comfortable:

Every time one of us reprimanded the other's children, we would let each other know and explain why we found it necessary to so. At the same time, we had to actively decide to trust the other person's judgment and good intentions. We both also recognized that it was very difficult for us to handle criticism of our children without always being defensive. Hence we should also remember to confirm with each other that we liked each other's children. The "proof" for this was that we made sure we praised each other's children when they did or said something nice, pleasant, or loving.

Implementing the above method may sound a bit exaggerated, but it really helped Jegwan and me in situations that otherwise could have gone wrong.

One day I noticed that I no longer had a stomach-ache when Jegwan reprimanded my boys. I was completely at peace with my mother hen instinct and no longer needed to be defensive when Jegwan raised his voice. I had reached my goal. I had completely let go and trusted 100% that he wanted the best for my boys. What a feeling of relief.

It took me a while to get there. Hopefully many of you will get there a lot faster, but it was just so hard to let go and trust Jegwan to reprimand my children without my supervision.

7.4   When the fusion parent fails or is inadequate, in your opinion

In the process of living as a blended family, it is inevitable that we as parents get into situations where we feel that the fusion parent's reaction towards our children leaves something to be desired.

As the parent we are allowed to criticize our children without any consequences, but if the fusion parent does the same, they might as well put on armor right away, because they might be in for a fight. A parent might automatically question the fusions parent's intentions by asking leading emotional and manipulative questions. We do not hear the fusion parent's answers to our questions unless they are compatible with the answers we expect to hear.

My own story

As I have described earlier, I had great difficulty in dealing with situations where I thought Jegwan overreacted and had been unfair to my boys. He even expected that I should listen to his "nonsense" arguments. I felt like this was a waste of my time.

Patience and tolerance are not two words I use when describing myself. On the other hand, I never hesitate to admit that I could always see his underlying intentions in those situations where I got mad or was hurt.

I "knew how things were" and offered him my help in those cases where he clearly had not understood what I believed was right or wrong. The strange thing was that he never took advantage of my unique offers. Jegwan could never get through to me as I played the role of "mom-who-is-hurt-on-behalf-on her-children," that is, until I was done being mad and my rational judgment began to work again.

I would then return with some reluctance to the situation and promise to participate in the experiment of "listening without interrupting to correct him." When I then listened to his explanation, it was never as I thought it "should be" so what should I do then? Should I say the magic word: sorry? I decided to let the "accused" have the benefit of doubt and practiced not thinking the worst as a starting point when Jegwan said or did something with regard to my boys that I initially disagreed with.

In such situations, the parent must try to show the fusion parent the necessary confidence by maintaining the belief that they had good intentions by reacting/acting the way they did and not holding a grudge. Also, it may be a good idea to distance oneself a little before listening openly to the fusion parent's arguments.

Charlotte Egemar Kaaber

> **Reflection**
> Throughout the process of achieving the necessary confidence with each other, the partners must demonstrate strong understanding, patience, and tolerance when one party repeatedly "fails" and accuses the other party of not having good intentions. If the accused party has the necessary energy to explain their true intentions, it will definitely shorten the path towards the goal. It is necessary that both parties learn to listen to each other and feel the emotions and reactions of the situation without being judgmental and conclusive. Both the parent and the fusion parent must make painstaking efforts to join in a mutual understanding without imposing distrustful and critical questions about the other's intentions.

Similarly, it is imperative to be able to forgive each other for the mistakes that inevitably will occur in relation to the fusion children. If the fusion parent is also a parent, it may help to remember situations where they made some missteps in the relationship with their own children. This may help them believe that the fusion parent's actions were based on loving intentions.

7.5 FUSION CHILDREN – ARE THEY THE REASON FOR ARGUMENTS?

When a fusion parent gets mad at their fusion children in front of the parent, it might not always be the children who are the real problem. The fusion parent might be subconsciously projecting their anger on the children in order to have a reason to justify their anger.

"How can I admit that I am actually jealous of the kids who are constantly stealing my partner's attention? I just can't say that out loud. It is also embarrassing, and I feel so belittled that I have become jealous of children! No, I'd better get mad about something quite specific that the "brats" have done. In addition, it is also possible that I've made the situation into something far

98

more serious than it actually was. I'll have to cover my back so I am ready to resist any apology from my partner."

How can we avoid this flawed situation, which not only damages the fusion parent's relationship to the fusion children, but also creates distance to the partner? Perhaps subconsciously, a lack of loving support and recognition is the reason for the fusion parent's irritation. One must then try to ignore all the negative and instead show the fusion parent love, care, and recognition.

If the fusion parent complains about lack of care, a "reinvestment" will soon pay off with a happy and smiling fusion parent who has regained the energy to care for the children.

If the frustration towards the fusion children turns into extreme anger and rage, it is important that the parent remembers that the children's acceptance of the fusion parent is fully integrated as part of their upbringing, so that this does not need to be addressed each time problems arise.

It is also important that the parent has honestly assessed whether the fusion parent is right in their "accusations." If this is not the case, the parent should step in and clarify the requirements they have for the fusion parent and their role. The fusion parent may have to be reminded that they, together with the parent, are responsible for creating a good relationship with the children.

The parent should not accept the fusion parent's criticism of the children's lack of care or interest in them. Children are so sensitive that they can clearly feel if the fusion parent does not like them or thinks they are annoying. If children are confident and excited about the fusion parent, they will also seek their company. If they don't, then they remain distant.

When all is said and done, it is important that the parent continues to show the fusion parent trust, that they still rely on the fusion parent's judgment of a situation, and that they want the best for the kids. Another, significant factor that may play a role in a strained relationship between a fusion parent and children, may be that the parent is tense and pressures their kids. Read more about this in the section: <u>5.7.3   Pitfall 3: Being tense and pressuring your kids</u>.

7.6   JEALOUSY AMONGST THE KIDS

Especially in the beginning of the new blended family life, jealousy among the children may occur. Children may behave very possessive towards their parent and take complete ownership of the parent. Children are afraid that the new siblings might "steal" their parent from them and/or the parent ultimately prefers the new fusion children to them. It is possible, depending on how old the children are, to alleviate their jealousy. The fusion parent and the parent can "practice" with the children by sitting with each others' children simultaneously. It gives the children a sense of "something for something": "You've borrowed my dad, but I have in return borrowed your mom. We're even."

When you have practiced this "exercise" for some time, children will begin to relax more. When the day comes when your child leaves the room to go play while your fusion child sits with you, you will know you have come a long way in alleviating the jealousy.

It requires great patience and understanding from both parent and fusion parent to overcome sibling rivalry, but as long as you are aware of the problem and do something for the child, it will be easier for them to deal with their feelings of jealousy. If the kids are older you can talk to them about how they honestly feel about having to share their parent or if they feel that the new fusion siblings take too much of the parent's time. You can also ask them if there is something important to them that you still need to do in order for them to feel loved.

7.7 THE FUSION PARENT THINKS THE PARENT "FORGETS" THAT THEY HAVE KIDS

As fusion parent you might feel that you need to remind the parent that they have children. A committed fusion parent might experience frustration if the parent does not want to see his or her own children. It's difficult to understand why. And when the children do finally come to your house, time is too short to really get to know them, which creates great frustration.

If the fusion parent feels the need to work on enhancing the interaction with the fusion children, they must consider the role of the partner with regard to the kids and not their own parental role. The parent's perception of their role can be very different from the fusion parent's role, and therefore it is important not to judge each other. It is also important not to criticize the parent for their apparent lack of commitment to the children. The fusion parent should instead ask the parent what kind of relationship they really want to have with the children. Maybe the fusion parent will find out that the parent has never really thought deeply about their role or has been critical of how they are as a parent.

The parent may find it difficult to respond to the question immediately. They might have forgotten themselves along the way, and now only see themselves as a parent, not an individual. The parent may have accepted the rare interaction with the children as status quo, and must therefore be given time to find themselves again in hope that their emotions reappear. The fusion parent should kindly remind the parent that they must invest time in seeing the children if they want a good, close relationship with them in the future. The fusion parent should also be willing to support increased contact and actively assist with practical issues. The fusion parent can help the parent think of their values and highlight all the good traits the fusion parent has, which can then be passed on to the children.

7.8   WHEN THE KID/KIDS GET DROPPED OFF AT THE OTHER PARENT'S HOUSE

Most parents know what their ideal drop-off/pick-up situation should look like: A friendly chat with the ex over a quick cup of coffee while you update each other about the children's lives, then giving the ex a friendly hug, and affectionately kissing the kids goodbye.

Unfortunately, this beautiful picture is a rarity as there may be many emotions to take into account. It is not the only the parent's relationship to the ex that determines how and what can be done, but also both the partner of the ex and the fusion parent who can have a decisive impact on the solution for the issue, which you as a parent have to accept. Regardless of which deal you finally end up with, it is certainly a requirement that we as parents ensure the children's well-being.

Let us take a look at this fictional example:

The other parents refuse all contact with the parent and demand the children be dropped off in front of their house. They will neither see nor speak to the parent when this takes place. In this situation, the parent must ensure that the responsibility for children is properly assigned to someone at home ready to greet the children when they are dropped off.

If the children are young, the parent should never accept this kind of arrangement. Although the door is open and the parent can see the children entering, it is still important that the parent gets some kind of feedback about their arrival from the adults inside the house. A parent must receive this acknowledgment from the other parents, and not simply trust that the open door means some one is at home. What if the other parents were gone for five minutes? In those five minutes when the children were alone, something could have happened to them. If it is not possible to get feedback or acknowledgment, the parent should not drop the children off and the parties must instead find another option, for example through a third person.

Many parents might choose a kindergarten or school pick-up/drop-off as an alternative. If the two sets of parents cannot stand the sight of each other, then this alternative will not work and they may choose to have the grandparents and/or friend help. Setting a time frame of around fifteen minutes where the child is in third party's custody ensures that the transfer of responsibility for children is done in an orderly manner. Whether you as a parent would be willing to involve a third party is a completely different issue, but it may be a good and safe solution if the two of you do not wish to see each other.

If the fusion parent has an issue with the ex dropping off the kids, the parent should use this opportunity to tell the fusion parent that they must simply accept it as part of the baggage that came with the parent.

If the fusion parent is also a parent, they will probably eventually recognize and respect the parent's decision as to what is best for the children with regard to drop-off/pick-up.

Sharing information about the children between the two sets of parents is described in following sections:

- 5.7.4   Pitfall 4: When "weekend kids" come into the newly existing family
- 8.5   The kids are "messengers" between the parents

7.9   BEING PRESENT AND CREATING SECURITY

Closeness and security might be hard to come by in the fusion family. These factors must be present in all types of family configurations, but it is harder to create such an environment for the children in the blended family.

In the nuclear family the children usually live with both parents, which in most cases is in itself a safe and secure environment. In a fusion family, the children live with one parent plus a fusion parent, which does not automatically give the children the usual sense of security. It's all new to them: new people, new routines, new habits, etc., nothing is as it used to be. All these new circumstances and people can create great insecurity in the children since their everyday life no longer is as it used to be.

It is therefore important that parents in the blended family make a great effort to restore the sense of security that children need in order to thrive. This means that both the parent and fusion parent are present and engaged in the conversations they have with the children.

When the children talk about their day, it is important to listen actively. Let the fusion parent talk to their fusion children about their daily lives – this is a good way for them to get to know each other. Since children do not always have well-developed situational awareness, they might choose to speak with you when you're busy and can't be interrupted. In this situation, the fusion parent should tell the child that they don't have time right now and therefore can't listen properly, but that they will soon. You don't want to listen without really listening, saying "hmmm" and "okay" – the children can feel that. When you do seek out the child, they will know that you are now ready to listen very carefully, giving the child the feeling that you are honest and an adult who takes them seriously. Similarly both the fusion parent and parent's affection towards the children is important to their sense of security and feeling loved.

As a complement to being present and providing reassurance, the parent and the fusion parent may choose to incorporate some of these ideas I have described in the book:

- 6.1.1 Gift 1: Creating traditions in the blended family
- 6.1.2 Gift 2: Making ordinary things important

- 6.1.3 Gift 3: A fusion parent can find his/her own niche
- 6.1.4 Gift 4: Doing something special with the fusion child
- 5.7.7 Pitfall 7: Is it okay to treat the kids differently?

7.10 IT'S OKAY FOR THE ADULT TO APOLOGIZE

As an adult in a fusion family it is imperative to apologize when necessary, not only to your partner but also to the children. It is inevitable that you will have arguments and you might say something you come to regret. When you come to the conclusion that it is of great benefit to the family's mental health to give them an unreserved and sincere apology, follow up by giving them the real explanation for your reaction. It's of great value to the other adult and to the children that you acknowledge your flaws and are willing to admit to not being faultless.

When adults can apologize to children, it helps the children to not blame themselves if they make mistakes. The children see that adults are not always perfect, and therefore will not expect to always be perfect themselves. Being able to apologize to the family will help create a healthy balance for the requirements and expectations that both children and adults have of each other.

7.11 STARTING OVER WHEN SOMETHING HAS GONE WRONG

My own story
The concept of a Fresh Start when a situation goes wrong is something I have "invented" and introduced in our blended family.

I think everyone has experienced being in an excellent mood only to have it plummet to anger or despair in less than ten seconds. I have often felt this when all six of us get home at the same time. We swarm through the door dropping bags, laptops, backpacks and everything else while questions fly through the air: "Can I play on the computer?" "What are having for dinner?" "I'm hungry, when do we eat?" I completely stress out, and I before I know it I'm in a bad mood, complaining about everything and everyone. Situations like these repeated themselves, until one day when everything went wrong again, I shouted to my entire family: "Everyone STOP! This isn't good, we have to start all over again!" The children and Jegwan looked at me and asked what I meant by that. I ordered them all to put on their jackets again, pick up their bags and sit in the car. I told them that we had to start over again and see if we could all do better this time.

The children thought I was crazy and giggled a little. We again swarmed in the door, but this time we were aware that we would behave better. We couldn't help laughing a little at the silly idea and were all in a much better mood. To this day, I just have to say, "Oops, something went wrong," then we just start all over again and make another attempt.

Reflection
It might feel like it takes extra energy to reverse a situation that has gone wrong, but once you succeed you will find out that you are using less energy in the long run.

8. LIFE IN THE FUSION FAMILY WITH THE OTHER PARENT AND POSSIBLE PROBLEMS

8.1 FUSION MOM/DAD VERSUS THE OTHER PARENT

When you yourself have children, you develop unconditional love for them. From diapers to later listening about their first failed love affair. Knowing your children well and often purely intuitively, you are the best person to advise and guide them in the challenges they will encounter throughout life. It is the parent who lovingly helps the children develop into an independent adult. This is the absolute responsibility of the parent.

So, it is not always an easy task to be a fusion parent to someone else's children. When we get to know our fusion children, their path has already been mapped out by their parents, which in itself can be challenging for the fusion parent. It's a difficult balancing act with great risk of undue interference. Where are your invisible borders as a fusion parent when you have assumed responsibility for your fusion children, and what can you do without risking a conflict with the other parent?

There is no doubt that the most optimal solution would be if we as fusion parents can get in touch with the "real" parents and clarify their position on the fusion parent role, which can then define their limits. By doing this, you will then not have to constantly evaluate your role and ask yourself, "Am I allowed to do this, and what will the "real" parent say?" The fact that you took the "real" parent into consideration can make it possible to relax in your role as a fusion parent.

8.2 FUSION PARENTS OFTEN LIVE LIFE IN THE "DANGER ZONE"

There are an incredible number of topics where you are "at risk" in your behavior as fusion parent. Some of them are:

1. Do you discuss the "real" parent's decision if you disagree with them?
2. Is it okay to buy things for the kids?
3. If the kids want the fusion parent to participate at parent/teacher meetings, should you do it?
4. If the kids want the fusion parent to participate in school events, should you do it?

Comments on issue 1:
I think we as fusion parents have the right to be heard even when we do not agree with the real parent's decision. However, I do not think it is necessary if the outcome of the parent's decision has no direct impact on the children's well-being. In cases where the fusion parent really feels it is of great importance to modify the real parent's decision, the fusion parent should give their opinion to their partner, who can then judge whether they will take it into consideration. The fusion parent and the parent must agree before they contact the real parent. If the fusion parent and the parent do not agree, the fusion parent should give in and let parents decide.

Comments on issue 2:

Buying things for your fusion children might be a very sensitive issue, and of course is done with the best intentions. The real parent's financial situation versus the fusion family's financial situation may be very different, thus the possibilities are different when it comes to buying for the kids. The optimal solution in this situation is to ask the real parent if they are okay with you buying things. On the other hand, it's ultimately you who decides whether any consideration should be taken or not.

Comments on issue 3:

At school parent/teacher meetings, it's usually the children's mother and father who are involved. Agreement from the two parents is necessary before the fusion parents can participate. One of Jegwan's and my friends told me with a big smile that he, his wife, his ex and her boyfriend showed up for a parent/teacher meeting at his son's school. It's really nice to hear that it is possible.

Comments on issue 4:

If we look at the worst possible situation in order to evaluate whether it's really necessary to consider all parties involved, it could look like this:

Example
The children come home from kindergarten and announce that they want everyone to come to their school and watch them in a theatre play. Panic spreads among the adults – who is entitled to participate?

When the children are with their father on the day of the play, he believes that it is he and his girlfriend who should attend. He then calls their mother to inform her that he and his girlfriend will go. The mother does NOT agree and therefore proclaims that they are her children and that she intends to attend the play. The father feels he can't deny the mother's rights, but has no desire to go to the play with her alone. So he decides to stay home, though inwardly he knows that the children would be happy if he attended.

What is this really about and what do the children want in this situation? Can we cautiously conclude that it's impossible to take all parties into account all the time? If the adults could learn to put their own feelings aside, everyone would then be able to participate and fulfill the children's wishes by simply being in the same room together and watching their play.

There is probably only one thing to do when children ask the fusion parent whether they will participate in an activity, and that is to answer honestly, "Yes, I would really like to and I am delighted that you asked." As long as you base your decision on the child's wishes, the other parents cannot accuse you of anything besides not taking them into account. The children must hold the adults themselves accountable if they choose to stay away from events. However, it is important to remember that the responsibility for these complicated situations lies with the adults.

8.3   INTERVIEW WITH A FUSION DAD

Thomas lives with Anne and Anne's daughter Eline, who is three and a half years old. They have lived together for a half year.

Questions to Thomas: What is your biggest challenge as a fusion dad to Eline?

Answer: *The biggest challenge is that I had to set my own needs aside in deciding how things are done. I also think I would reach my limit sooner if Eline had been my own child. Anne and I have discussed this, but she does not believe there is a difference. I get easily upset when things go awry.*

Sometimes I'd like to be able to sit for two hours and read a book, but I just can't do that without feeling guilty. Anne has often offered to take Eline somewhere so that I can have some peace and quiet. I never accept that offer because I'm not comfortable when I can't stand the same things as her biological parent – it feels to me like giving up a bit. Maybe it's okay... maybe it is not entirely unreasonable to relax for two hours. Then there is also Sunday morning when you just can't sleep in anymore.

Q: What is your preference in participating in social events that include Eline's "real" father?

Answer: *I think I would want to participate. I've been to some social events in Eline's kindergarten, including barbeques and lectures, but I do not think Eline's father was invited. When Eline gets older and expresses that she wants her father to come to her birthday parties, she should be allowed to do so. Although I have to admit that I would rather NOT sit next to Anne's ex-husband at the dinner table.*

At Eline's last birthday she had one birthday party with us and one with her father. Eline would like to have had her father here, but I think he was on vacation. I've actually been in a situation where Anne invited him for dinner because Eline wanted him to come. But that didn't happen. We can easily meet in public places, but when he comes to my house I feel that he somehow enters my territory. Not that I have something against him, he is a nice guy and all, but it just feels wrong to me.

I try also to express in front of Eline's father that I am fully aware that he is her biological father, and that I am not a threat to him. I am friendly and courteous, and I ensure him that there is no doubt that he is the father, and that I am always secondary. I don't want to take over his role as the father and he should not feel threatened.

Q: How would you handle a situation where you felt that Anne did not have time and/or energy for you because of Eline?

Answer: *In our everyday life, we spend 2-3 hours alone together when Eline has gone to bed. Sometimes Eline comes into our bed at night, which irritates me a little even though I very well understand that Eline needs the reassurance. I would just like to have Anne to myself, so we can have some private time. It was not something Anne* *had thought about before, as she was accustomed to being alone with Eline.*

Anne adds: *Eline eventually slept in her own bed until we were told how important it was for children to feel emotionally secure. So Thomas gave up and said that she could sleep in our bed again. Thomas actually compromised. But now we hope that she does not need to so often.*

Thomas adds: *If I don't get a good night's sleep, I become more irritable. I don't want Eline to sleep between us, because I want to hold Anne at night. I even went to sleep on the couch because I got so mad and I could not sleep.*

Question to Anne: Do you feel that Thomas as a fusion dad also should be consulted on issues regarding Eline, or is it purely a matter for parents?

Answer: *I certainly think that he should, otherwise how he would be part of her life? I think that we are both parents to her and that Thomas should have a say as well. We discuss what is good for her. Thomas also attends parent/teacher meetings. If I expect Thomas to be included on equal terms with me, he should be consulted on issues regarding Eline. I also ask Thomas for advice when it comes to the school she goes to, etc.*

Q: Do you see Thomas and his family as part of Eline's family?

Answer: *Yes, I do. They live very far away and so we are not together with them very often anyway. Thomas' parents looked after her for the first time on Saturday, and it went well beyond all expectations. They do everything to make Eline feel that she is their grandchild. I feared that they would not like her, but there is no doubt that they DO like her a lot. Thomas' parents treat her the same way they treat their "real" grandchildren. That they have deeper feelings for, and know* *their own grandchildren better than Eline is quite understandable. It is what it is.*

Thomas comments: *I do think there is a difference. I think there is a difference in how much they love their biological grandchildren versus Eline. I think there is something about the biological… that you will love the biological child more. The paradox is that my parents now have the opportunity to be with Eline more often than with their biological grandchildren because they have moved abroad. But, I think there is a difference and there always will be.*

Q: What is your opinion on whether Thomas should participate in social events and/or birthdays for Eline when her "real" father also is present?

Answer: *When we lived together he never participated in such events, so I must admit I have not offered to have him participate now. He has never been interested in participating in these things. Not because he is not allowed to come. Personally, I prefer Thomas to be present at the events. If Eline's father were also there, I feel that I should make sure he was comfortable about the situation. If Eline wants her father to come to her birthday, of course she is allowed to have him there.*

Q: If you were to give good advice to a parent who lives with a boyfriend/girlfriend who does not have children, what would it be?

Answer: *It is a good idea to work together with the fusion parent, and to expect that the fusion parent will take responsibility on equal terms with the parent. They should act in unison towards the children and represent a common position on important issues. I think this provides reassurance.*

It is also important to be forthcoming towards the new fusion parent, and make sure that there is also room for their opinion. Responsibility and influence follow hand in hand. Similarly, you must prioritize and have alone time together without the children.

My evaluation
Thomas' role as a fusion dad

It is important to be honest and accept if you need some alone time in peace and quiet. This is true both for the fusion parent, but certainly also for the parent. We cannot be there for others if we do not have resources and energy to give. It seems worth remembering when we feel guilty about our lack of ability.

Thomas feels like he fails when he cannot do the same things as Anne. However, it would be to the benefit of all parties if he accepts Anne's offer of some peace and quiet for a few hours, so he can recharge and fully be present as an adult in Eline's life.

If he chooses to do something with Eline, without taking time to re-energize, the quality of what he does will be half-hearted and he might find himself thinking: "I'd rather be sitting and reading in peace and quiet."

So if you have a choice, choose what you need and do it with a clear conscience. You will of course return with more energy.

We parents tend, almost consistently, to put ourselves aside for the children's sake, because we cannot afford to be so selfish and do something for ourselves, BEFORE we do something for the kids. The question is: Do we really do something nice for the children in this 'energy deficient' way or do we really just do it for ourselves in order to feel good? Doing things wholeheartedly without expecting anything in return, creates the ideal situation for both the kids and the adults.

If we ask our children, I am sure they would prefer that we do that we need to do and are happy, rather than forcing ourselves, which often results in irritated adults who have had enough.

We do not have to feel guilty about taking breaks, to gather strength again to be a good parent to our children.

Thomas' role as Eline's fusion dad vs. Eline's biological dad

A sense of belonging is strengthened when Thomas chooses (and is allowed) to participate in events at Eline's kindergarten, rather than staying at home. He takes his role as a fusion parent seriously and participates on equally term with Anne.

Anne's ex-husband does not participate, but even if he did, it is still healthy and creates a feeling of belonging in the fusion family when you insist on participating in social events and thus take an active part in you fusion child's everyday life.

If you do not want to or are not allowed to participate in your fusion children's activities, you can easily get a feeling of loneliness and that you stand outside it all reduced to being an observer of your partner and his/her children's life.

When the social events with the kids are taking place on neutral ground with the biological parents, and when parents and fusion parents are not forced to interact with one another, but can sit at opposite ends of the room, then I do not think it is overstepping the boundaries for what you can do as fusion parent.

If the children are older, they do not have to choose whether they want the fusion parent or biological parent present. The children can safely ask both sets of parents if they want to participate in the social event.

8.4 DIFFERENT SETS OF RULES AND THE KIDS BEING ABLE TO SPEAK FREELY ABOUT EXPERIENCES TO BOTH SETS OF PARENTS

There may be a very big difference between the rules and routines set by the respective parents, and it may take time before the kids remember how things are done in the two families. It can be really hard for the kids to go from one parent's house to the other, and it is important that we parents remember that it is often confusing for them to have to deal with the two different rule sets. The children may need the adults to remind them of how things are done from time to time.

Whether children can talk freely about their experiences with their respective parents is unfortunately directly connected to the emotions that are present among the adults. The fusion parent's possible jealousy over the parent's past can come into play. If one parent has hurt by the split up and has not moved on with their life, they might not want to hear the children talk enthusiastically about the time spent with their ex and the new fusion parent.

The children's enthusiasm may reinforce the other parent's feelings of inadequacy. The phrase "If it's so great to be away from me, then just move there," should only be used one single time so that the kids understand that the parent does not share their joy about the other parent.

Another not so unusual situation is when the parent who was hurt emotionally by the split up tells the other parent "to go to hell" in front of the children. In this situation, the children know not speak with too much enthusiasm about the other parent.

Another factor that may also come into play is the fusion parent's jealousy of their partner's past. In this instance, the fusion parent cannot tolerate the children's praise of their partner's ex. If the kids tell the fusion parent about an experience they had with their mother/father, and the fusion parent says nothing or seems very uninterested, the children will feel that they shouldn't talk about it again.

We as adults must set our emotions aside and let the kids talk freely about their experiences with their respective parents without facing any negative consequences. If we cannot handle this, it's time to take a look within ourselves and honestly evaluate whether we are acting fairly, as the children should NOT end up as scapegoats for the adult's chaos of emotions. Parents have no other choice other than to rely on each other's ability to be critical while also having a healthy discernment towards things the children tell them. In the role of as a fusion parent, it is especially important that you trust the "real" parent to listen critically to the children if they complain about you.

As a fusion parent, it is also important to be self-critical while also being confident when it comes to defending what you have said about the real parent. If you mess up, be honest when confronted. Never tell the children "Do not tell your mother/father," or "Do not tell on me." These are phrases that only convey that you aren't honest and don't have good intentions. If we feel the need to use these phrases towards the children, it's time for a deep "self-inspection" in which behavior and action must be adjusted carefully in order to prevent using these phrases in the future. It is important to remember that children do not gossip about what they experience, they just talk about how they feel in different situations.

Here is an example:

If your child comes home and says: "I am afraid of A" it is not the words that are important, but the emotions that the child felt in this context and how these feelings arose. If the real parent finds it necessary to confront the fusion parent with situation, it is vital for the child that the fusion parent does not hold a grudge against the child and that no subsequent victimization is made. The fusion parent must listen and try to understand the feelings they created for the child in that situation and allow the child had to speak about the experience with their mother/father.

The fusion parent should consider the feelings they created in the child and take responsibility for them by ensuring that it does not happen again. Subsequently the fusion parent must apologize and tell the child that they are sorry that the child was frightened and that it was not intended, and that they will do their best so the child won't feel that way again.

> **Reflection**
> Adults should make an effort to show kids, both by words and actions, that the kids are free to talk about all their experiences and feelings – and that all their emotions are legitimate and without consequence regardless of content. Good ways to show the children this is by providing neutral and interested questions about their experiences with the other parent and ask how they feel in different situations in a non-interrogational way.

8.5   THE KIDS ARE "MESSENGERS" BETWEEN THE PARENTS

If the parental communication is poor or nonexistent we must, as parents of minor children, not impose the responsibility on the children to be messengers between the adults. Children can become incredibly stressed if they have to remember messages going back and forth from parent to parent.

Many parents may think that short messages or messages about certain topics are okay, but to a child any message may still be stressful. A good example for this is about the time kids are being picked up/dropped off. It seems simple, but may be stressful if your or your ex are on a tight schedule.

In this situation it is advisable to introduce the standard picked up/dropped off schedule, so that the child and both sets of parents know what to abide by and be able to plan around. Parents do not need to schedule different pick up/drop off times from time to time and the child should not have to spend energy on remembering or asking about when he/she will be picked up or dropped off. In addition, you need to allocate sufficient time, so that the child does not feel stressed out and rushed.

It's therefore important that issues regarding the kids are communicated directly between the two parents. If the two sets of parents can not/will not talk to each other, they may choose to write emails. Written communication is better than no communication at all.

If there is an issue that the other parent should follow up on, take care of it–it's better if you can get it out of the way before the kids arrive. It will be more comfortable this way, as the kids will find out that their issues already have been handled. The children then don't have to constantly explain themselves or start over with stories, because the adults already know all about what happened, and therefore are immediately able to continue to follow up where the other parent left off.

8.6 WHEN THE KIDS DON'T THRIVE WITH THE EX AND THE OTHER FUSION PARENT

It is a very difficult situation to be in when children express to you that they aren't thriving or that they dislike being with the ex and the other fusion parent. How do we handle the situation? And when do you act on the situation with the other parent? You should try talking to children about the experiences and feelings they have when they are with the other parent. The parent should try to find the true reason why the kids do not like to be with the other parent.

The parent must also pay close attention if the child gets angry and blames himself or whether the child is distancing himself from the situation by responding with anger against the other parent. If the child blames himself, the parent should try to get the child to talk and open up about his emotions. If you feel that you can't get through to the child, I recommend that you seek professional help.

However, if the child distances himself from the situation and turns the anger toward the adults, he is telling you that he does not feel responsible for the situation at the other parents' house. The child feels that it is the adults' fault, not his, and is a healthy way of reacting.

If the kids are projecting their anger onto the other fusion parent and not the parent, this may be due to the following conditions:

1. The parent has pressured the children and estranged them from the fusion parent
2. The children feel that the fusion parent treats them differently from their own children
3. Although they make the same mistakes, the children feel that the fusion parent scolds them more than their own children
4. The children feel that the fusion parent does not give them the same care and attention that they give their own children
5. The children feel that the fusion parent does not like them.

If anger also is directed at the parent, this may be due to the following conditions:

1. The children feel that the parent spends too much time with the fusion parent's children and forgets about them
2. The children feel that the parent always sides with the fusion parent's children in conflicts and no one listens to them and their version of the conflict
3. The children feel that the parent never listens to their feelings, but consistently says that the way they feel is not right

If you have the above challenges in your fusion family, you may encounter the children reacting very strongly or violently. Something is not working for them when they are with the other parent, and they express this when they come home to the blended family. The children may have made a great effort to put a lid on their emotions while they were with your ex, but the moment they come home to you they explode. It may seem unfair that the children choose to save it all until they come home, but it may also actually be an expression of confidence – when they're with you they react freely and express their feelings, and know with certainty that they are loved.

If you ever have a chance, you should try to talk to your ex about it without being accusatory and judgmental, and with the principle that all of you want the best for the children. When you speak with your ex about a sensitive topic, remember not to push any buttons and instead try to be open and solution-oriented. You can possibly ask the ex if they have any idea about why the children do not enjoy being with them. You can also add that you'd like to help improve the situation. If necessary, the parent can reassure the ex by explaining that you still are supporting the children's contact with them and that you do not intend to change the agreement just because something is not working the way it should.

The parent's goal with the ex should be peace and the possibility of improving the situation with children instead of preparing themselves for their "next move." The "next move" is very important, because this is when things go very wrong between the ex and the parent. If the relationship is very bad, the ex will spend all their energy getting ready for a battle against the parent because they fear that the parent is trying to change arrangements with the children, or in the worst case, terminate all contact. The parent must make an effort that the situation does not end up being a competition between parents as to who is the most competent parent.

If your children do not seem to thrive when they are with your ex, I recommend that you be very cautious before attempting to change the arrangement the children have with their father or mother. Children are indeed incredibly loyal and loving to both their mother and father and will often prefer to be with their beloved parent instead of with the "stupid" fusion parent. Children often develop an ability to shut off what they do not like and accept that "that's just how it is" when they are with their parent. As long as the parent can feel and see that the kids still have a good relationship with the other parent, and still have good memories and moments, I think the parent should try to maintain a friendship. Regardless of how much you would like to help your children thrive, you must remember that you can not change the facts about your ex. You can support and listen to the children when they express their feelings, and make sure that they feel loved.

Again, it is worth remembering that whatever the outcome of a battle is, it can cause enormous emotional damage to the children. It is therefore incredibly important to choose your battles with your ex carefully.

8.7   WHEN THE KIDS CONFRONT THE PARENTS

Children who have a hard time being with the other parent will very often remember incidents that occurred earlier in their lives, but neither then nor at this age can understand and/or find plausible explanations for what happened. Children will always remember the strong feelings they had in that regard. As described in the previous section, you cannot interfere with what happens at the other parent's house but you can listen and support your children. The parents in the fusion family must assess whether the children are old enough to confront the other parent themselves.

If the child previously was left to be with the fusion parent because the parent had to work a lot, the child might feel that the parent did not want to be with them. If the parents in the fusion family believe that the child is mature and strong enough to confront the other parent with their feelings, they may suggest the child should do so. The child might initially not want to and may be afraid of how the other parent will react. The fusion family can support and motivate the child to implement the confrontation by listening to them and legitimizing the child's feelings. The fusion family must also be willing to be confronted with questions, accusations and anger.

Whatever the reason is/was for why children do not thrive, they will get older and one day see the adult in a different and broader perspective that goes beyond the role of parent/fusion parent. With age, the child will get a better understanding of their parents' personalities, values, and priorities in life, along with clarity about the way the parents chose to live their life. This new insight may help the child find the cause of their previously incomprehensible past experiences and feelings.

Reflection

Fusion families who have children who have had or still have problems can help motivate them to make necessary confrontations when the time is right for the children. This way, the parents can actively help the children deal with their emotions and experiences and not carry their anger with them into their independent life as an adult.

8.8 WHEN THE KIDS TALK ABOUT BAD EXPERIENCES WITH THE EX

My own story

Initially, I found it incredibly difficult to say and do the right thing when my boys came home from their father and told me of an incident or a reaction that they were not able to understand.

I was committed to always backing up my ex about what was happening at his house. I consistently defended him and assured my boys that they had either misunderstood or perceived it wrong; then I explained to them how it all "really happened."

I felt very loyal towards the boys' father and their fusion mom, and at the time I thought I handled things in a good way. I didn't question anything about them. Almost by reflex, I always said, "No sweetheart. It isn't true. That's not how it really is, because... blah, blah, blah." Until the day my oldest son got furious with me and shouted, " I AM NEVER GOING TO TELL YOU ANYTHING MOM because you always say that the way I feel isn't true!" I stood there totally speechless while my son stared at me in anger, with a defiant face, ready for what his "wise" mother now would say. I pulled myself together and muttered, "Sorry sweetheart, I'm sorry." I had to think carefully about how I now would handle this new and unfamiliar situation. It suddenly dawned on me that I had been undermining my son's discernment, intuition and emotions, which I in all other aspects tried to strengthen and develop. I had been telling him that all his accumulated observations and feelings were non-existent and pure fabrication. No wonder he didn't want to tell me anything any more – I wasn't listening to what he really was saying.

I concluded that I had to distinguish between the different situations the children would tell us about. In some situations I could still manage the way I used to, while other situations demanded that I listen and be objective. If I agreed with the children about their anger or hurt feelings, I now answered, "I understand you're angry/upset." Since you are not responsible or liable for the way things are with your ex, you must instead recognize the children's observations and feelings without judging your ex.

8.9 FUTILE ATTEMPTS IN "EDUCATING" THE EX AND FORGETTING ABOUT YOUR EXPECTATIONS OF THE EX

It can be a very difficult balancing act not to push your limits and interfere in issues with the ex, such as abiding by the rule: What goes on in our fusion family is our business and what goes on with the ex's family is their business. I think we get the best results with our ex if we live by this unwritten rule. When you want to talk to your ex about the children, it is helpful to remind yourself that there is a reason why you are no longer with them, and that what went wrong at the time can very easily go wrong again.

Since you know the ex's strengths and weaknesses, you can easily activate the same old problems. Both parties can fall back into the same stereotypes. The battles you choose to have with your ex should be chosen carefully, taking your fusion family into account. You can try to put all the old feelings behind you and look at ex as if you met them for the first time. You can choose to treat your ex as a new business partner and see if you can establish a professional relationship where personal feelings aren't involved and instead focus on what is needed in order to solve the problems regarding the children.

The weekend bag with the dirty clothes can, for example, be a source of great irritation. When the children come home from the other parent's house with the bag full of dirty clothes, the parent may think that the ex should have washed the clothes before they sent it back. The other parent might think, "I see my kids so little, so I will not spend time washing their clothes when they are here." You can choose either to expect to get the dirty clothes back and be okay with it, or to give children some extra clothes that they can keep at the other parent's house.

It's hard to avoid having expectations of your ex and their contributions in relation to the children, especially if you live relatively close to each other. You expect your ex to invest the same amount of energy in the children as you do. If there is an event at school where it is obvious that you must participate, you expect your ex to do the same. If the ex for some reason chooses to be absent, you may feel disappointed on behalf of the children.

Since this issue often matters a great deal to the fusion family, I think it will help if you lower your expectations. Retain the original agreement, but give the other parent the option of participation. It may be a good idea to create a mail folder for notes and miscellaneous information to which both sets of parents have access.

8.10 ESTABLISHING INDEPENDENCE

My own story

In order to make everything flow, Jegwan and I planned our life in great detail. We explained our schedule to our employers as we lived in two different areas of the island and both worked in the capital of Copenhagen. Mondays and Tuesdays, when the children were not at our house, we could then compensate for our employers flexibility by working longer hours if needed. We had all the pieces together, but this also meant that we're very vulnerable to changes in the schedule. We were very dependent on our respective exes' ability to sustain the schedule, and this dependency sometimes created a lot of pressure. We therefore decided that we would try to create a situation where our blended family could still function even if there were changes in the schedule. We made this happen when my ex had to go abroad and my boys stayed with us for two months – we were still able to function in our everyday life.

To achieve this flexibility in everyday life you might have to change the circumstances around your everyday routines. You might need to find a high school student who can pick your child up and stay with him/her until you get home, or you may choose to take turns with a friend picking up/dropping off the children to and from day care or school.

If possible, you and your partner might have to change your work schedule or ask to work flexible hours.

If you need to have flexibility and independence, let me ask you a few questions:

What does it take to achieve this feeling of independence?
Why is it important for you to achieve it?
What does it give you and your family if you achieved it?
What you can change, cancel, or add in your daily life, in order to be independent?
What you can do today to get closer to this feeling?

Being flexible will give you a great sense of independence, knowing that you no longer have to rely on your ex and that everything will work out regardless. If you are disappointed in your ex's effort or lack thereof, maybe you should do something extra yourself. Your common denominator, which determines how things should be done in a child's life, should be to do whatever it takes. Both sets of parents have to take responsibility for their choices.

This is very important for the children in the blended family. If your ex does not have a new partner who can take over the obligation of purchasing a gift on the children's behalf, then the fusion family has to undertake this task. The children will be sad if they found out that they had no gift to give. If the blended family does not want to spend money on the other parent, the children can make a gift for them. It is essential that there is something for children to give to the other parent. If for some reason this is not possible, the parent in the blended family has to ensure that the ex's family members provide a gift on the children's behalf.

Allow me to give you some ideas for gifts that children themselves can make with a little help from you. I hope that you will like the ideas, or can look at them from the children's perspective:

Younger children

- Color a page from a coloring book and together wrap it nicely.
- Make a drawing, which you roll up and put a beautiful ribbon on.
- Design a bead plate in a pretty pattern or write "mother / father" on it.
- Make discount cards for foot massage performed by the child for mom/dad.
- Create gift certificates for house work e.g. the child will help emptying the dishwasher five times.

Older children
- Create beautiful colorized sketches
- Make discount card for massages performed by the child (I got that from three out of four children, but have unfortunately already used them all up.)
- Make discount card for gardening/house work/ shopping /cooking.
- Create gift certificates for breakfast in bed on a Sunday morning.
- Arrange a beautiful bouquet of flowers from the garden or from a field.

It is worth thinking about the incredible value there is in this action. It really builds a bridge between the two worlds in which the child interacts and it shows that you fully recognize the other parents household. Have fun-let the creativity flourish.

8.11 WHEN THE EX HAS A NEW PARTNER AND THE EX'S PARTNER CAN HURT AND/OR BENEFIT THE RELATIONSHIP TO THE FUSION FAMILY

When ex gets a new partner, it is necessary to inform the blended family so they have the opportunity to support the new relationship and prepare for the changes that will happen if the partner moves in and becomes a new fusion parent for the children. Basically, you have to trust the ex's choice of their new partner. The ex has been through the same considerations and hopefully has made sure that the new partner is willing to assume full responsibility and care for the children. Likewise, the parent must trust that ex's new partner has fully accepted that the relationship with the children has first priority, and wishes to establish a loving and warm relationship with their new fusion children. When communicating with the ex, the parent must always mention the new partner in positive terms.

The relationship with your ex, and the agreements you have, may change the moment the ex gets a new partner. The ex has gone from being single to now suddenly having a new partner who also has an opinion on the arrangements and the circumstances surrounding the children. As a parent, as I mentioned before, it is important to have a positive attitude toward the children and help introduce them to the new partner.

Your cooperation with your ex can change radically, both in positive and negative directions.

Positive direction:

If the relationship with your ex with regard to the children has been marked by their ill-concealed bitterness, it can improve the moment your ex meets a new partner. The negative energy your ex spent on you might be minimized or, at best, completely disappear. The ex will probably be very conscious not to show bitterness over your failures, since it definitely would not be a good starting point for making the new relationship work. The new partner also has the opportunity to look at the relationship between parents objectively and constructively, and directly/indirectly improve the cooperation and communication concerning the children.

If communication between the parents is non-existent, the new partner can choose to become the coordinator for the fusion family. The advantage of this constellation is that the new partner is not emotionally involved and therefore not influenced by the old stereotypes that made that parental communication come to a halt.

Negative direction, example:

Suzanne and her ex had established a good working relationship around their daughter. They handed her over to each other at the doors with a short description of what had happened in their daughter's life lately. This had worked perfectly until the day when Suzanne was told by her ex that she no longer would hand their daughter over at the door, but further down the street. Suzanne could only find one explanation for this change, namely that her ex's new girlfriend was jealous of her.

Suzanne was furious that her ex did not step in and explain to his new girlfriend that he sets the agenda for their daughter. If the new girlfriend couldn't accept this, she would should hide in the house and cover her ears and eyes. In this case, it was difficult for Suzanne to have faith in her ex and believe that he wanted what was best for their daughter. However, she understood that her ex felt compelled to take his new girlfriend into account – but he should have been more critical. Suzanne would not disappear from their life just because she was further down the street. Suzanne would always be a part of his past and he should have reminded his girlfriend of that and NOT agreed to change a relationship that was working well.

When the ex has a new partner whose presence results in changes in the existing agreements, the parent should only agree to them if they do not affect the children's well being. If these changes are harmful to children, the parent should stick to the existing and effective agreements and not accommodate the ex.

8.12 INTERVIEW WITH A FUSION FAMILY

Dianne and Michael have been dating for two and a half years. They split up at one time, but are now moving in together. Dianne has two kids: Martin, 14 years old and Emily, 11 years old. They live with Dianne and see their dad every other weekend. Michael also has two kids: Mark, 10 and Mia, 12. Michael has the kids every other weekend at his vacation home, which is fifty miles away from where Dianne and Michael live.

Questions to both Michael and Dianne: What is your attitude toward parenting/reprimanding each other's children?

Michael: *Great. Dianne does not say anything unjustified, and if my kids feel hurt they let her know.*

Dianne: *Michael has shouted at Emily right in her face because she teased him. I said to Michael that he just couldn't do that. My opinion is that you first give the child a warning. You do not start by shouting.*

Michael: *I gave her two warnings that day.*

Dianne: *Okay, I didn't hear that. Otherwise there hasn't really been anything, but it is clear that since we spend more time with my children, I'm more alert about how things are said, especially to my daughter. Michael's kids listen to what I say. When we were on vacation this summer, I said something to Martin. He's a big guy and he just pushed me away. It's because we have grown children. If the were children younger, they might perhaps listen better. I let this episode pass, but had it been something big and important, I would have said stop. Their upbringing is already formed, so we don't spend a lot of time on changing it.*

Q: What has been your biggest challenge meeting a new partner with children?

Michael: *It has not been a problem for me. I just took part in their lives. We have disagreed on some points. Sometimes I thought Dianne was not strict enough, other times I thought she was too hard on them. So I said that to her. Table manners mean a lot to Dianne and I have a little more relaxed attitude. So we ended up compromising.*

Dianne: *What has been hardest for me is that I think too much about it. I was very shocked to discover that I lacked the flexibility that I thought I had. There are aspects of my personality that I had no idea existed and which I actually do not want to talk about. I also had trouble understanding the environment Michael came from. It is very different from where I came from. In the beginning of our relationship, I was also very pushy towards Michael. I wondered about the way he handled things. Michael does things differently than I do. I had a hard time realizing that. There were things I thought were really strange, in particular that they did not celebrate birthdays together.*

Michael: *Dianne also thought it was strange that I only saw my children every other weekend.*

Dianne: *You have many differences when you enter into a new relationship with children. I think we try to get the best out of it, both strengths and weaknesses. Michael has been very focused on our differences. I try to take advantage of our differences. Michael is lazy and I am energetic, which means I have to slow down. Conversely, Michael uses my energy to get fired up and get things done. It important to find the right balance and remember what you are passionate about and what you want. When you sit around a table with four children, I especially can't expect Michael to hear my signals. I must instead communicate my needs to him. The longer I'm in it, and now that the kids are older, I think it is actually very nice. I often ask Michael if he has heard from his kids. I try to keep up with their lives as well. When he comes home I am ready with questions, but when Michael is tired, I wait.*

Michael: *I just have to relax first when I get home.*

Dianne: *I am interested in their lives and would like to know whether they had a great time. I'd also like to spend more time with them by staying at the vacation home, even when it's winter. Then we can be together more often.*

Q: How do you function in your daily life?

Dianne: *When we come home from work, we take time to just sit down and look each other in the eyes like sweethearts. Before, I would go directly into the kitchen and start cooking because I could easily hear what the kids and/or Michael were saying. It is much better taking your time and slowly doing practical things. It's different when you take your time.*

Michael: *Emily sits and does her homework while Dianne cooks. Maybe I'll help Emily with her homework so this way we are together.*

Dianne: *I certainly had to get used to Michael taking a nap for 15-20 minutes on the couch when he came home from work.*

Q: If you had to give a new fusion family some good advice, what would it be?

Dianne: *If the family has small children, I think the adults should be a little more relaxed. Be a little more indifferent as to whether the house is dusty and cluttered, or whether the children skipped the bath they should have had.*

Michael: *Being human is the most important thing!*

Dianne: *In the beginning I think it is important, if you live close to each other, to not think you have to be together all the time. You have to take time to walk in the woods and then make hot chocolate… just be together. I don't think you should expect to be together 24-7. Sometimes I think that can cause problems if you expect it. You must plan a little. You can't expect, when you bring four kids together, that the four will be friends. They won't. They are siblings and fusion siblings. Fusion siblings can hate each other just like ordinary siblings. I think you have to create situations where children can choose to join or not, depending on their age. If you have small children, they obviously have no choice, but if you have older children, let them choose to participate in the planned events or not.*

Michael: *Some weekends I have only one of my kids. It is really good for our relationship and I am much closer to the child now than if I had them both.*

Dianne: *There is no simple solution. What works for one family, does not work for the other.*

My evaluation
Parenting/reprimanding each other's children

Dianne and Michael have been trying to find a compromise on how and which way the children should be brought up. When should we reprimand them and when can we be a little more lax about things.

Upbringing of one another's children is a source of perpetual conflict and bickering, so therefore it is important to talk about this topic early on in the relationship.

The clearer you explain yourself to one another about where you are coming from and are accustomed to, the easier it will be to find a way which will work for your family. It is important to ask yourselves these questions and know the answers: What is important to me? Why is it important?

Maybe you will find that something you previously reprimanded your kids for is no longer important. Maybe you have projected issues and situations from your own childhood without thinking much about whether it works for you now and whether you think it is important.

The day your partner reprimands your kids, you might by instinct act defensively, regardless of the content. It is a completely natural and expected response. It is part of our protective instincts as parents.

With this in mind it is important that you are aware of whether you need an explanation from your partner, so you do not make up your own version of why he rebuked your children. Ask for answers to what you need to know, so you are at peace with the situation immediately, instead of having to live through and analyze the situation again and again.

With time and trust in your partner's good intentions, you will slowly be at peace with his/her partaking in the upbringing of your kids.

It feels good and at the same time it is a relief to leave old parenting patterns and habits behind and together find ways which promote the well-being of your fusion family.

8.13 THE GRANDPARENTS DISCRIMINATE AND "FORGET" THE FUSION KIDS

It can be difficult for the respective families of the fusion family to accept and/or remember that there are suddenly more grandchildren they have to deal with. It may take time before the family becomes accustomed to the new situation. Therefore it may take some time before the family treats the new fusion children the same way they treat their own grandchildren. The fusion family must give their families time before they begin to tell them how they should act.

In fusion families where only one set of children stays on weekends, it can be difficult for grandparents to know how to act in relation to the "weekend kids." Because the grandparents don't see them often they don't know the children as well and therefore do not relate to them in the same way they relate to the "real" grandchildren. For some fusion families it may well be acceptable that the grandchildren only buy presents for their own grandchildren. In other families, this behaviour is the source of great debate, since the parent might be hurt and feel that the grandparents discriminate against and do not accept their children.

If the fusion parent gets hurt and can't accept this discrimination, the parent should talk with their parents and explain what is expected of them in the future with regard to the fusion children. When confronted, the grandparents may actually see be relived to receive guidelines. They might have had a hard time of their own trying to figure out the right way to act.

In fusion families where both the adults have their children each week, the adults may expect the grandparents to behave the same way towards both sets of children. If this does not happen by itself, both the fusion parent and the parent must talk with their families and explain/remind them not to discriminate amongst the children. The same applies to invitations to family gatherings. Everyone in the fusion family should be invited. If this does not happen automatically, the fusion families should set this requirement for the families.

References

Manning Inspire ApS inspired "Tools of the Fusion Coach."

Acknowledgements

Thanks to the reader of The Fusion Family. Thank you for investing money and time to seek help, inspiration or advice for your own family situation. I am very happy about that. The more families who create "ripples in the water" and show the way to a loving and well functioning family life, the more we are to inspire and instill hope.

I smile at the thought that perhaps there is a fusion family out there that have introduced some of my ideas and hopefully welcomes the outcome. I am much obliged.

To all who have supported me in publishing this book. Thank you for your belief in both my idea and in me.

Thank you to my husband Jegwan Kaaber for your support and wise contributions. There would not have been a book without your great ideas. Thanks for your patience, love and eternal faith in me and what I can do.

Sweet Michael Herluf-Staack. Thank you for the lovely cover, and thank you for spending time with me. I am so proud.

Jeanett Knudstrup thanks for your great effort in proofreading the Danish version. You are fantastic.

Thanks to my wonderful fusion children, Oscar and Andrea, for your interest in finalizing this book. A special thanks to you, beautiful Andrea Kaaber, for being proud of me while exclaiming:

"YES, you can now buy a book which my fusion mom has written." Also, thanks to my wonderful boys Nicklas and Jonas for your interest in the book.

A big thanks to my parents Lis and Erik Egemar Olsen for your support and pride in me. A special thanks to my mother for your proofreading and for your faith in me and my idea, that there's a need for this book.

Also a thanks to my father in-law Henning Kaaber for your wise words, "Charlotte, you should write the book as you think it should sound. You should not listen to anyone else."

Thanks to my wonderful sisters-in-law Maria Kaaber Wright, Anne Kaaber, and their wonderful families. Thank you for your sparring, support and care. I love being in your company. Let that happen more frequently.

Jegwan's beautiful niece Anne-Sofie Kaaber, thanks for your wise and inspiring contributions.

To all my wonderful colleagues in the "Tunnel and Metrofield"-thanks for all the inspirational talks and inputs you have given me along the way. Thank you for your faith in my idea.

Thanks to my friend Dorte Munthe Kjeldsen for your support and for helping me stay focused on my goal. Your projects are interesting as well…!

Thanks to Vivien Lundsgaard-Hector for translating the book from Danish to English for "finding my voice" and also thanks to Holly Kreiswirth for proofreading the English version.

Meet the Danish Fusion Family and meet Charlotte on <u>www.fusionfamily.us</u>. For Updates on Charlottes activities and new products subscribe to the newsletter.